EVER SO NEW

Cheryl Phillip-Jordan

Bladensburg, MD

Published by Inscript Books
a division of Dove Christian Publishers
P.O. Box 611
Bladensburg, MD 20710-0611
www.inscriptpublishing.com

Scriptures, unless otherwise marked, are taken from THE HOLY BIBLE, KING JAMES VERSION, public domain.

Inscript and the portrayal of a pen with script are trademarks of Dove Christian Publishers.

ISBN: 978-1-7375177-7-1

Copyright © 2022 by Cheryl Phillip-Jordan

Cover art by Errol 'EJ' Mc Kenzie

All Rights Reserved. No part of this publication may be reproduced, stored in a retrieval system or transmitted in any form or by any means – electronic, mechanical, photocopy, or any other – except for brief quotations in printed reviews, without the prior permission of the author.

Printed in the United States of America

To my family, whose patient support proved invaluable.

Table of Contents

FOREWORD	1
THE WINNING SIDE	2
HE IS THERE	7
THE CROSSINGS	12
THE BURNT OFFERING	18
MOTIVES	23
THE GIANTS	27
RECOGNISING THE TRUTH	30
AN HEART TO PERCEIVE	35
THE QUICK FIX	40
ACHAN	46
INHERITANCE	50
FOLLOW CLOSELY	56
THE CHOSEN	61
ASAHEL	65
CORRECT OFFICE	70
SAMSON, THE LOSER	74
PURITY	80
THE PROVISION OF GOD	85
FEAR	92
UNANSWERED PRAYERS?	101
VISION	108
OBEDIENCE TO GOD	112
DRY BONES	120
THE JOURNEY OF JONAH	124
RELEVANCE	129
FIRST AND ONLY	132

FOREWORD

This book presents a look at Old Testament accounts and their relevance to everyday life. As we examine characters and events recorded in the Old Testament, we realise that human beings have not changed, and neither has God.

Although stern, harsh judgments are common in the Old Testament, they seem largely replaced by mercy and grace in the New Testament; that is, until the book of Revelation.

Often neglected, the Old Testament is a treasure of knowledge that proves valuable as we live in our modern world. As you delve into these individual accounts, may you discover the beauty and the relevance of some of our well-known and lesser-known Bible stories and characters.

The Old Testament was never meant to be ignored and slighted the way it is today. It is not possible to love and serve One with whom you are not acquainted, not for want of information, but simply for lack of interest. The Old Testament teaches us about the mercy of God, the goodness of God, the faithfulness of God, and the judgment of God.

The Word of God is precious, valuable, and priceless in its entirety. May the Old Testament be given the attention it truly deserves.

1

THE WINNING SIDE

(Exodus 14)

A great battle was about to take place: the children of Israel against the Egyptians. It looked as if the children of Israel were in for a beating, and the victory they had won when they left Egypt was about to be snatched from them. If you were a betting person, you wouldn't put any money on them. They were recently freed slaves with no fighting experience and no weapons. Manual labour was all they knew. They had herds and flocks, but livestock is not used for fighting battles. They had gold and silver, but you can't fight your enemy with money (Though many persons in our world today hold that view, these types of problems are not resolved simply by throwing money at them).

Money can be used to hire professional help, but the children of Israel could not hire an army to fight for them. It was just them and their enemy out there in the wilderness. The odds did not favour them.

Egypt was a mighty nation. Their kings were powerful and their army well-trained and well-equipped—all the chariots of Egypt, including the best 600 and captains over every one of them. It was the best equipment plus the best fighting men of a mighty nation against a group of ex-slaves. Their leader, Moses, was no fighter either; he had killed an Egyptian in his younger years, but he had no military training. But God was on their side.

God + the weakest army *OR*

God + no army *OR*

God + a bunch of frightened ex-slaves *equals* a mighty fighting force.

But the Egyptians had no way of knowing that.

In today's world, we all have our battles. It may be a sickness, a family problem, a financial situation, or something you cannot tell anyone about, but God on your side makes you a mighty fighter.

There are times when the enemy observes our

progress and speaks about us. We are going along our way, not knowing that we are being monitored. In the book of Job chapter 1, when asked to give an account of his activities, Satan tells the Lord that he has been going up and down the earth, apparently checking out everyone. In 1st Peter 5:8, we are warned to be sober and vigilant because our enemy, as a roaring lion, is walking around looking for someone to devour.

In this account, the enemy, Pharaoh, knew where the children of Israel were and assumed that they were trapped. The enemy is watching us, observing our victories. He knows where we are, and he plans and strategises the attack. But God knows everything, including the details of the enemy's plan. Satan's plan is not just against us but is against the One who is leading and protecting us, who created us, and who created the heavens and the earth.

The plan of the enemy against our families and us cannot prosper. Those attacks may be well-planned, but they are doomed to fail because our God is fighting for us. The attack may be well-timed and well-coordinated, but God is on our side. We need to lift up our eyes and see the Lord is with us and not just see the enemy (2 Kings 6:17).

When we get fearful, we cry out to the Lord, not like the Israelites cry out and complain, but we cry out and trust.

This experience brought out the worst in the children of Israel. They wished to surrender. In fact, they wished they had never been freed. What an insult to the Lord! How quickly they had forgotten the chains of slavery, the murder of their babies (Exodus 1:16), the abuse (Exodus 1:13), and their cries for deliverance (Exodus 3:7).

Why would anyone want to serve the Egyptians when they could serve the Lord? Why would anyone want to remain in bondage in Egypt when they can be free in the promised land? Why would anyone want to live under conditions where their sons, from birth and through childhood, were prey (Exodus 1:22) and their daughters could only look forward to a life of abuse and servitude? There is an alternative. Serving God and raising children to do the same (Joshua 24:15) is the way to go. Some are making unfortunate choices today.

We are not going to die in the wilderness, though sometimes it looks and feels like it. God will make a way where there seems to be none. He will make a way where no way exists according to our human understanding.

In Exodus chapter 15, the children of Israel sang songs of victory. We like to sing songs of victory, but we do not want the battles. Unfortunately, there must first be a battle in order to have a victory. The Red Sea crossing took the children of Israel to a new level. There would be other enemies in the future, but Pharaoh and his army were gone, never to return.

We cannot fight all our enemies at once, but we

can trust the Lord to overcome them bit by bit as we progress in Him.

2

HE IS THERE

(Exodus 14)

The Lord, in a pillar of fire by night and a cloud by day, was leading the children of Israel through the wilderness after their release from Egypt. Pharaoh had a change of heart after they left and decided to give chase, intending to capture and re-enslave them.

The Lord moved from His usual position in

front of the children of Israel and went behind them. This had never happened before (Exodus 13:22). It may not have looked good to the children of Israel. Sometimes when we are in a hard place and cannot see God leading us, we panic. But He may be behind us to give us protection. When God does something new in your life in the middle of trouble, it is a clue that something big is on its way. He is fully aware of what is going on, and He is taking action.

He is behind us, keeping the enemy at bay while we obey Him and keep marching on. When you are marching forward, it is difficult to fight an enemy that is behind you. You have two options. Either stop marching, turn back and fight or you continue forward and allow the enemy to sneak up on you and hinder your progress. Either way, you are slowed down, and it will take longer to get to where you are going.

By day, the Lord went before them, leading them by a pillar of cloud, which was no ordinary cloud. It was not a cloud God plucked from the sky, nor was it one that He made and positioned in front of them. For the Lord was in the cloud (Exodus 13:21).

There are other instances in the Bible where the presence of God manifested Itself as a cloud. When Solomon dedicated the first temple, the priests were unable to stand to minister because the cloud of the glory of the Lord filled the house (1 Kings 8:11). Our Lord ascended into heaven in a cloud as His earthly ministry ended (Acts 1:9). In the book of

Revelation, chapter 11, we are told that the two witnesses sent in the end times will be killed, resurrected after three and a half days, and ascend into heaven in a cloud.

The cloud in the wilderness was easy to see, for there is usually a cloud shortage there. Whatever is in short supply, the Lord can provide in abundance. This cloud was not little, like a man's hand (1 Kings 18:44). It was not a sign of things to come. It was a pillar, large and well defined. It made a bold statement: '*I AM HERE.*' A large cloud was needed to provide shade in the wilderness where there were no shady trees.

At night, the pillar of fire stood out brightly in the dark. There was no failing to see its glow or feel its warmth. The wilderness can be quite chilly after dark. God is always relevant and has perfect timing. The presence of God has been represented by fire in many other instances in the Bible. Moses saw a burning bush (Exodus 3:2), and Mount Sinai had both a thick cloud and then fire as the Lord spoke to His servant (Exodus 19:16-18). The prophet Elijah was taken up to heaven in a chariot of fire with horses of fire (2 Kings 2:11), and that prophet had called down fire from heaven on more than one occasion (1 Kings 18:38; 2 Kings 1:9-12). In the vision of Isaiah the prophet, the temple was filled with smoke (Isaiah 6:4).

The wilderness, then, is just one of the occasions when the Lord showed His presence as a cloud, smoke, or fire. But we know that even when we see no visible manifestation of His presence, He is there (Psalm 139:7). Despite that, we only feel assured of a positive outcome of our situation when the Lord shows up in a way we can see.

The three young men who were thrown into the furnace by the enraged King Nebuchadnezzar not only survived the experience but had no smell of fire on them (Daniel 3). The unbelieving king was shocked to see them walking around in the fire, and even more amazing was the sight of a fourth man in the fire with them. The king recognised Him as the Son of God, but were the three young men in the fire privileged to see the fourth man? We do not know, but we know that God was there all along, but later chose to make Himself visible to the king.

The same condition that can be vexing and a hindrance to one camp can be a blessing to the other. The same Lord (the angel of God) was a cloud and darkness *in the night* to Pharaoh's camp but was a pillar of fire to the camp of Israel. In uncertain times, God can brighten your path and provide comfort and warmth, even as others grope in the darkness. It may be the economy, a difficult domestic situation, a less than desirable neighborhood, or a job that is not offering what it should (either in terms of money or career fulfillment and satisfaction); the Lord can and will be what you need when you need it. He provided direction, comfort, and shade by day, and warmth and light by night.

If you are experiencing difficulty, it may just be a set-up for the Lord to show His power. For when the breakthrough comes, when the healing comes, when the deliverance comes, when the answer comes, when the blessing comes, there will be no doubt who is responsible. **IT IS THE LORD!!!**

What does the situation look like? Are you walking in His light? Are you getting the correct view? Make sure you are in the right camp, for it determines your perspective and your destiny. The camp of Pharaoh was destined for destruction, while the children of Israel were earmarked for victory.

3

THE CROSSINGS

The Red Sea
(Exodus 14:15-28)

At the Red Sea, the children of Israel were terrified of the enemy pursuing them. This was the enemy that had enslaved them for 400 years (Genesis 15:13). They were ex-slaves, newly freed, but with a lot of Egypt still in them. Any problem that arose, their first response was, *Let us go back to Egypt. It was better there* (Exodus 14:11-12; 16:3; Numbers

14:4).

There were no priests. There was no ark. They had not fought any battles yet. In fact, Moses told them, *"The Lord shall fight for you, and ye shall hold your peace"* (Exodus 14:14). The Lord knew their anxiety, their fear, their apprehension, and their lack of fighting skills. Everybody remembered the experiences of slavery. That was all they knew.

At the Red Sea, they felt trapped. There was a physical barrier ahead and an enemy in hot pursuit behind. But God told Moses to lift up his rod and stretch his hand over the sea to divide it. The children of Israel would then go through onto dry ground. It happened just as God said. Further, as the enemy tried to follow them in the Red Sea, the waters returned, drowning their enemies. The way God makes for His people is not intended to be used by their enemies.

The Red Sea was the first big challenge they met after leaving Egypt. Many of us can remember our first big challenge after giving our hearts to the Lord. Some do not make it past the first hurdle and go back. The parable of the sower and the seed (Matthew 13:3-4) explains this first-test syndrome. In this parable, the birds of the air (the enemy) quickly devoured the seeds that fell by the wayside. These seeds (the Word) never got an opportunity to grow.

The Jordan
(Joshua 3:8-17)

At the Jordan River, it is a new generation

(Numbers 32:11). There is also a new leader, Joshua. Moses is dead. Unlike the case at the Red Sea, no enemy is pursuing them. Rather, their reputation has preceded them (Joshua 2:10). Even in the absence of modern communication, all the nations have heard of their progress and victories. Now they are in pursuit of the enemy ahead. They are off to battle. They have learned to fight.

Joshua did not receive any instructions from the Lord about stretching a rod over the river. In fact, he may not have had one at all. Rather, he instructed the people to sanctify themselves because the Lord would perform wonders the following day. This came after a three-day rest near the Jordan (Joshua 3:2). Amazing things can happen after three days.

The priests were to bear the ark. The Jordan was in flood stage. This was the worst possible time to cross. Surely God could have arranged the crossing during a more convenient season.

The power of God is not restrained by times and seasons. Your miracle or breakthrough can occur at the most difficult or unlikely time of your life. Even looking at a river in flood stage can be frightening. Imagine crossing it on foot. The feet of the priests had to step into the water. What were they feeling? Fear, anxiety, confidence, excitement? They were human beings. The rest of the congregation crossed on dry ground without ever wetting their feet. The priests were required to take the first bold steps into the flooded river. There are times when the spiritual leaders have to step out in faith, at the command of the Lord, ahead of their followers.

Similarly, when the priests came out of the Jordan and stepped unto dry land, the waters of the Jordan returned and continued to flood as they did before (Joshua 4:18).

At the River Jordan, God instructed Joshua to send 12 men, one from each tribe, into the parted river to collect 12 stones. These were to be used to make a monument on the other side of the river so that they and their children would never forget the crossing (Joshua 4:1-8). At the Red Sea, haste was important, and there had been no time to collect souvenirs. Besides, the children of Israel were just starting their journey, and the promised land was some distance away.

As you mature in the Lord, as you grow in Him, He will require more from you—more prayer, more faith, more fasting, more meditating on His Word. The children of Israel went from holding their peace and having the Lord fight for them (Exodus 14:14) to fighting kings and capturing their land. Sihon and Og, kings of the Amorites, had been defeated by an army that now knew how to fight (Deuteronomy 2:31; 3:3).

The Jordan was a river, not a sea. But it did not matter. The same God who divided the Red Sea was also able to part the Jordan River, even in flood. God had them cross the Jordan right near to Jericho, their next target (Joshua 3:16).

God could be positioning you in the right place at the right time, though it may not appear so. No enemy would be expecting an army to cross the Jordan when it is in flood. It was an unexpected crossing, at an unexpected time, in an unexpected manner.

At a normal flow, the Jordan could be crossed on foot. The children of Israel could have crossed the river at the fords, where everybody else did. A ford in a river is a shallow place where crossing on foot or by vehicle could occur. However, the enemy would have been expecting them at the fords. When Rahab hid the spies on her roof, then sent them away, the military personnel pursued them as far as the fords then turned back and returned to Jericho (Joshua 2:7). They reasoned that if they had not caught up to them by then, they had already escaped to the other side of the river.

But God did not need fords for His people to cross the Jordan. He created a brand-new way – a way the enemy could not anticipate and at an unlikely time. God can do things in unusual ways, in ways that no one even imagined. He is God like that! For all wisdom dwells with Him (Colossians 2:3).

We have an enemy who is always looking for ways to defeat us. If the enemy knows our itinerary, he could plan and lay traps for us. In regular life, security experts tell us to change our routes from time to time in order to throw off any attacks being planned. That is why praying in the Spirit is so important, for the enemy has no way of knowing what we are praying and is unable to lay traps for us. Use the heavenly language regularly. It was given to us for our benefit.

4

THE BURNT OFFERING

(Leviticus 1)

The burnt offering is one of the five offerings contained in the instructions given to the children of Israel by God at Mt. Sinai. The other offerings are:
- Sin offering
- Trespass offering
- Peace offering
- Meat offering

Of the five offerings, the sin offering and the trespass offering were compulsory. By these, sin was temporarily covered by the blood of an animal. Sin must be removed or at least covered before man can start a meaningful relationship with God. Christ removed our sin when He shed His blood on the cross. Our Christian relationship with Him started there.

The burnt offering represents consecration, that is, giving it all to the Lord.

The animal to be offered, an ox, ram, lamb, or fowl, was to be slain at the altar. It could not arrive at the altar already dead or dying. Old animals which had outlived their usefulness were not acceptable. The animal had to be valuable and full of potential. There was never any chance of the animal being pregnant or in an unclean cycle since only males were sacrificed. Blemishes and imperfections were not allowed, and even the inside of the animal was examined before it was burnt.

The apostle Paul admonishes us to present our bodies as a living sacrifice (Romans 12:1). While deathbed conversions are possible, deathbed consecrations are not. This process takes time, and we must be alert and capable during this time. One of the thieves crucified with Jesus was converted on the cross. That was his deathbed. Though he was never baptized nor counselled, for there was no time, he was saved (Luke 23:43). We have been made clean by the blood of the Lamb. Our dirty, sinful selves cannot be consecrated.

Wild animals could not be caught and dragged to the altar of sacrifice in the way that domesticated animals could be brought. We must be willing to be consecrated. It cannot be done against our will. This process cannot be forced on anyone. Remember, it is a voluntary offering. No one can drag us to the altar of sacrifice.

The entire animal was burnt in this offering. This is a complete sacrifice. We must present our whole selves. We cannot hold back on God. There is a temptation to make it look like we are offering everything while quietly holding back part in secret, as Ananias and Sapphira did (Acts 5:2). We are tempted to offer our spiritual selves or our church selves while keeping our social selves, our financial selves, our emotional selves, and our sexual selves safely hidden away and reserved for some other use.

The burnt offering catered to all income groups. Only the wealthy could offer an ox; others brought a ram or lamb, and those who could not afford them brought turtle doves or pigeons. In the same way, the process of consecration is available to all, regardless of spiritual status, wealth, or position in church society.

Once we are willing to consecrate our lives to the Master, we must be willing to be taken apart. The animals being offered were cut into pieces at the joints; the parts were washed and then assembled on the altar before burning. Bones were kept whole. We must be disjointed before God, powerless and disassembled in pieces, and allow Him and His Word to divide us (Hebrews 4:12) and wash us on the inside before putting us back together and allowing the fire of the Holy Spirit to consume us.

There will be no room for bitterness, strife, poor attitude, racism, classism, and envy. We will be clean on the inside as well as outside. Yes, we can be saved, that is, have our sins forgiven and refuse to go the extra mile to be consecrated. But when we think of the great love Christ demonstrated to us, just the thought of His willing sacrifice should make us want to offer ourselves completely at His altar.

In the Old Testament, only priests were qualified to offer burnt offerings on someone's behalf (1 Samuel 13:9-13). But we have been made priests (Revelation 1:6). God loves to do things in threes. There is the Trinity (Matthew 3:16-17); we are body, soul, and spirit (1 Thessalonians 5:23); Jonah was in the belly of the great fish three days and three nights (Jonah 1:17); Jesus rose on the third day (Matthew 16:21), and during His earthly ministry, Jesus had an inner circle of three disciples (Matthew 17:1). We are the children of God bringing the sacrifice, we are the living sacrifice, and we are the priest officiating at the altar.

Christ presented Himself on the cross willingly. He did not resist. He gave Himself as a sweet-smelling savour (Ephesians 5:2). Christ was the unblemished sacrifice. His was a one-time offering. Ours must be repeated, since we are human beings.

The burnt offering was corporate and also individual. The corporate burnt offering was offered twice a day – morning and evening. An individual was free to bring his burnt offering whenever he desired. Groups and organisations must always be consecrated to God. It is a continual process.

Consecration is voluntary but desirable. It is a way of showing our love to our Lord and Saviour, Jesus Christ. Since He offered Himself freely and completely, we must be willing to do the same. Refusing to do so indicates a lack of love and appreciation for Him. It puts us in danger of slowly drifting from Him. It may also point to a spirit of pride when we think we are so spiritually mature that we do not need to revisit the altar of sacrifice. Undesirable elements accumulate unseen on the inside, and we are soon overcome by them. This explains the presence of spirits of anger, lust, hatred, and others among the people of God. While it may be possible to live an apparently successful Christian life without it, spiritual growth is stunted, and there is the ever-present danger of easily getting lost. May we regularly present ourselves at His altar and allow His spirit to examine us, not just on the outside where we and others can see, but more importantly, on the inside where danger hides.

5
MOTIVES

In Numbers chapter one, God gives Moses and Aaron specific instructions to number the fighting men of the children of Israel. Only fit, adult males are to be counted. That may seem politically incorrect in today's world. Then later, Moses is again instructed to number the people (Numbers 26). There was purpose in both these numbering exercises.

Later, when the nation is established, King David commits sin by doing the same thing, that is, numbering the people. What makes it right in Numbers chapters 1 and 26 and makes it a sin in 2 Samuel chapter 24? The answer is simple: obedience to God. We are not masters of ourselves; we belong to Him. Therefore, it is our duty to always obey Him. It is not that He changes, for He cannot change (Malachi 3:6) and, indeed, has no reason to, for He is perfect.

However, His commands and instructions may change depending on the circumstances. David was told different strategies for battle (1 Samuel 23:4; 2 Samuel 5:24), and the wise men were warned to return home by a different route (Matthew 2:12). In other cases, some were told to go to Egypt (Matthew 2:13), and in other cases, some were warned not to go there (Jeremiah 42:19). Of course, there are fixed values for adultery, idolatry, and the like.

The census in Numbers chapter one was necessary. These ex-slaves knew little about their numbers. They were going to receive an inheritance based on their numbers. Later, Moses sent out a group of 12 spies to search out and describe the promised land (Numbers 13:17). That mission ended badly, though they returned safely. It was while they reported to the rest of the congregation that they spread their unbelief and lack of faith, even as they admitted that the land was indeed prosperous and promising (Numbers 13:27). God wanted to show He meant what He said about them not seeing or entering the promised land (Numbers 14:29). Not only had they failed to believe God for themselves, but they were also able to win over the congregation to their unbelief. They were so convincing that the rest of the children of Israel, except Joshua and Caleb, reached the point of wanting to stone the faithful. The majority is not always right.

The second census revealed that none of the old, offending, unbelieving generations, except Joshua and Caleb, were alive (Numbers 26:64-65). Joshua and Caleb were the only ones who chose to believe what God said even in the face of strong opposition (Numbers 14:6).

Later, David had ulterior motives for numbering the people. He was trying to flex his muscles. He was saying to the Lord, "*Hey, I've got this. I can handle it. Look at how many soldiers I have. Let me see who I can defeat with an army of this size. Let me compare my army to the army of the enemy.*"

Though it started with the Lord being angry with Israel (2 Samuel 24:1), God knew the heart of David and influenced him to do the population count. In the same way that God hardened the heart of Pharaoh (Exodus 7:3) because it was already trending in that way (Exodus 5:2), God led David to number the people.

But David forgot that as a youth, as a shepherd boy, lacking weapons of war, lacking military training and experience, lacking the armour of a warrior, even lacking the age of a soldier, he was successful against Goliath. This giant, frightening on his own, was clad in armour, had weapons, and taunted daily the army of the children of Israel with what must have been a booming, bellowing voice (1 Samuel 17:4).

For the sin of numbering the people, there was swift judgment from the Lord (2 Samuel 24:10). So, it is obvious that one's motives are extremely important. The question is, why are we doing what we are doing? Is it because God said so, or is it because it feels good or looks good?

Our motives can change an act that appears innocent into a full-blown sin. Dire consequences may follow. While man sees our outward appearance, the Lord has a different picture, for He sees our heart (1 Samuel 16:7), and it may not be a pretty picture (Jeremiah 17:9).

6
THE GIANTS

By their sheer size and physical strength, giants come across as powerful. The first time that giants are mentioned in the Bible, they seem to have come about as a result of illicit unions (Genesis 6:4). Giants are always portrayed as something to fight. They are never shown positively and were not meant to be entertained or encouraged.

None of the giants in the Bible are friendly or helpful. They did not assist the people of God by performing tasks no normal man could do. Rather, they used their size to instill fear, create anxiety and panic, and prevent the people of God from enjoying what God gave them. Interestingly enough, there were no giants among the people of God. King Saul was tall (1 Samuel 9:2), and Samson was strong (Judges 16:3), but neither of them was a giant.

Some giants are bullies. Not content with being able to scare us by their mere size, they taunt us daily, keeping us submerged in fear (1 Samuel 17:8). All chance of victory on our side is gone because we are so wrapped in fear, we spend our time and energy finding new places to hide rather than planning strategies to fight. Hope seems lost when your entire life is focused on ways of hiding from the giant that bullies you. One giant, Goliath, kept an entire army paralysed by fear. That causes rational behaviour to go out the window. Daily life becomes centered on surviving the giant. Creativity is stifled, and life is reduced to a daily survival struggle.

One giant was a king. Imagine he already had the advantage of his physical size, added to the power of a monarch. He seemed unbeatable, yet he was defeated (Deuteronomy 3:11). Some giants come in groups so that their power is multiplied. The sons of Anak so intimidated the children of Israel that they were willing to doubt God Himself and rebelled against Him. Israel saw themselves as grasshoppers (Numbers 13:33) and lost their promise of inheritance and their lives because of fear of giants (Numbers 14:35). The word of God was stronger than the giants they saw (Numbers 13:2), but it seemed easier for them to doubt God than to believe Him. God knew there were giants in the land, but victory was still assured to His people.

Anything in life that causes you to lose hope, seems insurmountable, refuses to go away, and makes life intolerable, is your giant. Some giants push you to the brink of sanity and beyond. Giants are not concerned about your welfare; in fact, they try to reduce you to a whimpering coward. Never threaten your giant if you have no intention of fighting him. You may choose to peacefully co-exist with your giant, but that arrangement is not viable as the giant's aim is to conquer forcibly. You cannot sign conditions of peace with your giants, for they will not rest until you are completely beaten or even killed.

Giants may, without even saying or doing anything, intimidate you by making you see yourself as unimportant, foolish, or weak. Their mere presence causes insecurity and a lack of stability.

Debt, substance abuse and other addictions, and domestic abuse are just some examples of modern-day giants. Some remain hidden in closets; others are on bold display for all to see. Whatever your giant, know that it is not beaten by accident. Plan your action against your giant. Get professional help, pray, fast, and study the Word of God. Your Goliath may have just met his match.

7

RECOGNISING THE TRUTH

The ability to recognise the truth has always been important. The truth carries no variation. The truth is **THE TRUTH**.

There is a story of a bank that conducted a training course for its employees so that they would not be fooled by counterfeit money. During the training, the bank never exposed its staff to counterfeit money; rather, they were taught to identify the real currency. You see, if you can recognise the truth, all forms of the counterfeit will be recognised. It is counterproductive to intently study the counterfeit because it is easy to put new varieties on the market in response.

In 2 Chronicles 18, Jehoshaphat, king of Judah, made an alliance with Ahab, king of Israel. Jehoshaphat knew God. The alliance was ill-advised and almost cost him his life. However, he brought his fear and recognition of God to the arrangement.

After the two kings agreed to go into battle together, Jehoshaphat hesitated. He wanted to enquire for the word of the Lord. Ahab assembled 400 false prophets who prophesied what he wanted to hear. They even had props to complete the show, for one of them made horns of iron proclaiming that the Lord said, "With these thou shalt push Syria until they be consumed" (2 Chronicles 18:10). The scene was impressive. Both kings were clothed in royal apparel, sitting on their thrones while the 400 prophesied.

But Jehoshaphat was not convinced. He asked whether there was another prophet, for Jehoshaphat had been trained in the Word of God. In chapter 17, verses seven to nine, he had sent out the princes together with the Levites to teach the people the Word of God. Now Jehoshaphat himself knew that what he was being told by 400 prophets did not ring true.

The true prophet, Micaiah, was warned by the king's messenger of what he should prophesy. No one can dictate what a prophet should say. Micaiah, at first, acted as if he was going along with the pretense but was rebuked by the king. The king himself was aware that the words of the 400 were false. It was false but convenient.

In our world today, many are living a lifestyle they know to be filled with falsehood but continue to do so because it is easy and convenient.

There are many self-proclaimed prophets and prophetesses in our world today. How are we going to distinguish those who are true? If we study the Word of the Lord, if we are able to recognise the truth, the lies will be revealed. There is only ONE TRUTH. He is The Truth (John 14:6). Study Him and His Word (John 1:1). It is easy to distinguish falsehood if you are well acquainted with the truth.

The inability to recognise the truth can cause us pain and loss. Initially, the disciples in the storm did not recognise the Lord coming to them walking on the water (John 6:19-21). When they did, that recognition ended their storm and their journey. Had they not recognised Him, He may have gone past them (Mark 6:48). Some of our trials would end sooner if we were able to recognise Him and His actions.

The disciples on the road to Emmaus, after the resurrection of our Lord, did not recognise Him, though He walked with them for part of the journey (Luke 24:15-31). They found Him unaware of current events and assumed He must have been a stranger. They were depressed, feeling they had been let down. The One in whom they trusted had been crucified, apparently unable to help Himself, but they had hoped He would deliver the nation from oppression. Now all their hopes had been dashed to pieces. Yet, here was the Saviour walking with them, and they were not recognising Him. He even acted as if He intended to walk farther on past the village where they were headed. They insisted He stay with them, and their eyes were opened as they sat together for a meal. He vanished out of their sight. As they reflected, they realised that their hearts had responded even before they knew who He was. There seemed to be a spiritual connection operating before the one in the physical. The scriptures themselves are powerful, but the scripture explained by Him became even more so.

Is it possible that when we reach our lowest points, He is there with us, unrecognised?

The lack of recognition can cause a lengthening of our trials and an unnecessary worsening of our situation. We can lose faith and accuse Him of not caring, even while He is right there with us. Not recognising the truth can cause us to believe untruths and endanger our future (Jeremiah 20). The prophet Jeremiah spoke to his people, but they never believed him, choosing to trust in the words of lying prophets (Jeremiah 5:31).

King Jehoiakim was unwilling to recognise the truth. He threw the written Word of God into the fire, trying to destroy it (Jeremiah 36:23). But the Word of God cannot be destroyed (Isaiah 40:8).

Many have tried and failed. His Word is truth (John 17:17). If His Word could be destroyed, then so could He. But thank God, none of that is possible.

May we recognise Him, His presence, and His influence in our daily lives. That way, we will not be swayed by lies, misrepresentations, and other forms of falsehoods constantly being presented to us packaged as truth.

8
AN HEART TO PERCEIVE

(Deuteronomy 29:1-4)

The children of Israel had seen and experienced many things:
- The plagues of Egypt.
- The great deliverance and exodus.
- The parting of the Red Sea.
- The destruction of Pharaoh and his armies.
- Water gushing from a rock.

- Manna mysteriously appearing on the ground.
- A shaking mountain with fire and smoke

All symbolised the power and presence of God.

Yet in verse four, we read, *"the Lord hath not given you an heart to perceive..."*

It is not enough for us to see miracles or hear the powerful Word of God. Many individuals experience these but with different outcomes. It is God that gives us a heart to perceive and eyes to see. It is He that causes us to appreciate the work of God. It is He that causes us to desire Him.

Some of us think that if we had been alive when Christ walked the earth, we would have been so committed and dedicated to Him, unlike the scribes and Pharisees. In fact, we would have put Peter and those guys to shame. For they also had their moments of doubt, fear, and unbelief. Sometimes we feel that if an unsaved friend or relative had heard a particular sermon or seen that miracle, they would have run to the altar.

But it is God that gives the heart the ability to understand, to wish for, and to desire Him. You may say, *"Why, that is unfair if God gives one person the heart to perceive and does not give the other."*

Is it then that God condemns some to hell or to distant relationships with Him? We are not to be blamed if we don't want a relationship with God, then? No, God has given to every man a measure of faith (Romans 12:3). What have you done with yours?

From him who has not, will be taken away even the little that he has and to him who has, will more be given (Matthew 13:12). This is not necessarily referring to money, though we are well acquainted with the saying that the rich get richer and the poor get poorer. The parable of the sower and the seed (Matthew 13:3) shows that nothing was wrong or unproductive about the seed. Its productivity was determined by the ground on which it fell.

Let us contrast the attitude and spiritual progress of the children of Israel to that of the prostitute, Rahab. In Joshua chapter two, Joshua sends out two men to spy out the land of Jericho. God had promoted him to a position of leadership. He had been a member of the team sent out by Moses to spy out the land of Canaan (Numbers 13). Now this great man of faith was sending out spies. The two spies enter the home of Rahab, where they are saved from being captured and are also given valuable information about the nation living in fear of their approach.

Rahab did not live in a God-fearing land. She did not grow up in an atmosphere of worship to God. She had never seen any miracles. She did not know the Word of God. She was not being led by a prophet of God. She did not have a leader that consulted God regularly and to whom He spoke face to face. She belonged to a Godless culture, and, even worse, she was a prostitute. Yet, her heart was tender towards God. She had only heard of some of the miracles and mighty acts that the children of Israel experienced for themselves, yet her heart was full of desire for God. Rahab recognised the sovereignty of God. She knew her nation was doomed because God was not on their side, and it was only a matter of time before her city fell into the hands of the people of God.

It is not that she was being disloyal to her people. She had already pledged her loyalty to God. She was even prophesying. In Joshua chapter 2, verse 11, she said, "*...for the Lord your God, he is God in heaven above, and in earth beneath.*" Deuteronomy 4:39 records those same words being written into the law by Moses, who was now dead. Yet Rahab, who had never seen or read or even heard of the law, was quoting it. Her heart was already converted. She saved herself and her family (Joshua 6:17), was integrated into Jewish society, and was given the great honour of being in the genealogy of King David and of Jesus Himself (Matthew 1:5).

Women were not usually recorded in genealogies, but in the record of the generations in Matthew chapter 1, Rahab is found along with three other women. What an honour for a foreigner, a reformed prostitute, a woman from a conquered people. Against all odds, Rahab had a heart for God.

He will use what you have to give you a greater desire for Him. Similarly, He will use your lack of interest in Him to further remove you from His Kingdom. May we use wisely the initial measure of faith given to us so that it grows rather than diminishes to our detriment.

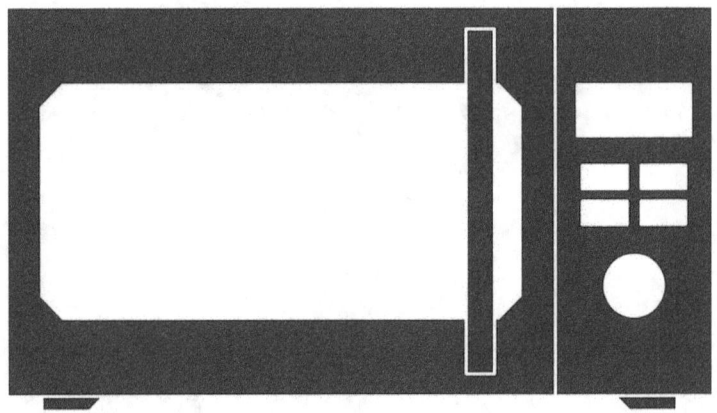

9

THE QUICK FIX

(1 Samuel 4:1-11)

Israel was on the battlefield fighting against a familiar enemy–the Philistines. How many times before had these two groups clashed? We can think back to Samson and think ahead to David and Goliath. So, this was not the first time, nor was it the last.

The enemy we are fighting today is not a new enemy. Whatever battle you are in is not the first and will not be the last unless God calls you home or returns to Earth. As Solomon observed, *"there is no new thing under the sun"* (Ecclesiastes 1:9).

The battle was not going well for Israel. They were losing. Four thousand men had already been killed. When the soldiers returned to camp, they were a defeated army. Discouragement, depression, and despair would have been the general mood.

If we are losing a battle, it could mean that we are not doing something right. For God is never off the job, is never wrong, declares the end before the beginning, is never asleep, and never makes promises and refuses to keep them (Numbers 23:19; Psalm 121:4; Isaiah 46:10). However, we know that there are battles where God is working out a greater purpose, for example, the persecution of the early church. There are also some things we will never understand in this world. But we know that in this battle, the children of Israel were way off-course.

Instead of seeing where they had gone wrong and calling the nation to a time of prayer, fasting, confession, repentance, sacrifice, and worship to God as they had done on a previous occasion (Judges 20:26), the elders or the leaders came up with a seemingly brilliant solution. Go, fetch the ark, and bring it on the battlefield. In other words, just bring God into whatever messy situation we have, and He will fix it.

This was the quick-fix solution, ready-to-go and "easy" service to God. How much time and effort was it going to take to repent and sacrifice and worship? Why waste that time and energy when it is so easy to just fetch the ark? At that time, Israel was not living a life pleasing to God. There was so much widespread idolatry that the Philistines did not know that the God of Israel was one God (1 Samuel 4:8).

An entire tribe had set up a false place of worship complete with priests and gods (Judges 18:30-31). There was also widespread sexual immorality, even among the priesthood (1 Samuel 2:22). God's people behaved like those of Sodom and Gomorrah (Judges 19:22-25; Genesis 19:4-9). When there are one or two cases of idolatry and sexual immorality, that is expected. But when it becomes the norm, when everybody thinks it is the right way to go and becomes institutionalised, we have big problems. Such was the state of Israel. These practices were no secret, yet it was felt that things would miraculously turn around once the ark was brought onto the scene.

How much time and energy would it take to repent, pray, fast, and read and study the Word of God? Surely, it is much easier and faster to pay a little money and get something to sprinkle around us, pin something onto our clothing, mumble a few words, or depend on the prayer of someone after we die to get us into Heaven. However, these are quick fixes, and, like bringing the ark on the battlefield, they may do more harm than good.

After the ark was brought into the battle, thirty thousand Israelites were slain. Things actually got worse for them. The arrival of the ark solicited different responses. Israel was excited, and the enemy was alarmed. That was a temporary response, though, for the enemy fought harder.

The Characteristics of Quick Fixes

- They are quick. Who does not love quick?
- They require little effort, spiritually. Israel thought they could keep their false gods in their hearts and summon the true God to work some magic on the battlefield.
- They are deceptive and dangerous. They give a false sense of security. You feel you are on the right road and do not need to do anything differently.
- They are popular. You do not get many people protesting about a quick fix. It always looks good and sounds like a good idea.
- Quick fixes glorify another – maybe the one who comes up with the idea or the one who carries it out (1 Corinthians 1:29).
- They reduce the need for God in our daily lives. It is: *"Don't call me, I'll call you. Just stand by. I've got this."* We seek to make God, the creator of the universe, a bellboy or a spare tyre.

When it comes to the things of God, a quick fix is never the way to go, regardless of how attractive it looks and how convenient it is.

The ark was captured by the enemy. That was meant to teach both Israel and the enemy a lesson.

Different lessons for different camps. Israel had to learn that God's way was the only way, while the Philistines had to learn that there was only one true God.

God had given specific instructions about the ark. It was not the idea of man. The design, dimensions, types of materials to be used, how it was to be transported and by whom, who was allowed to enter the area, and how often, were all set out by God.

Nowhere had God ever given instructions to bring the ark on the battlefield if things were not going Israel's way. The ark was not a charm nor a magic wand. They should have known that. Look at who was officiating over the ark on the battlefield: the two corrupt and sinful sons of Eli. They had been dipping their hands into the Lord's offering (1 Samuel 2:12-17) and practiced sexual immorality (1 Samuel 2:22), and they thought that they had spiritual authority?

God could have struck them dead as soon as they entered the area where the ark was kept. There was a specified time to enter that area. They were not struck dead, but that did not mean they had God's approval. Sometimes God allows us to do certain things, and we think He approves.

The ark was no longer in the tabernacle. The presence of God had departed, but the tabernacle did not disappear. How many of our churches remain functioning though the presence of God has long departed? The building remains, and the people continue to attend, but it is just empty rituals being performed.

Had this little scheme worked, the sons of Eli would have been heroes of the day. These corrupt and sinful priests would have been riding a wave of popularity that would have opened the door to more financial corruption and more sexual sin. Besides, God had already pronounced judgment on them, their father, and the coming generation (1 Samuel 2:27-36; 3:11-14).

Their father, Eli, had allowed them to carry on with their sins and never tried to correct them until it was too late (1 Samuel 2:23-25). Eli himself had long lost his spiritual vision, for he could not tell the difference between a drunkard and a soul in anguish before God (1 Samuel 1:12-16). His life ended at 98 years in grief when he fell back and broke his neck upon hearing of the capture of the ark (1 Samuel 4:18). The death of his two sons did not seem to trouble him as much as the news about the ark. He may have already given up on them since he had been warned by God on more than one occasion.

Eli was a leader who lost his way. Today, sadly, some of our leaders are losing their way. Spiritual leadership within the church is more difficult than secular leadership outside of the church. The enemy keeps our leaders in his crosshairs. Pray for our leaders and their families. They can find themselves being attacked by the enemy, by others being used by the enemy, by those outside the church, and also by those they seek to lead.

10

ACHAN

(Joshua chapters 6-8)

The story of Achan is a tragedy. It is a story about a man who would not wait. He decided to do things his way. It is a story about a disobedient, undisciplined, unbelieving, and selfish man.

He was just one of several thousands of soldiers in the army of Israel. Everyone else heeded the instructions given. All the silver, gold, and iron of Jericho belonged to the Lord. Everything else was to be burnt. One man out of thousands brought about untimely deaths (including his own) and caused embarrassment, defeat, humiliation, and destruction. He caused about 36 men to lose their lives in the battle of Ai, which was to be the next conquest. An entire army fled before the enemy, making the enemy appear stronger than it really was and making his army look weak, for Ai was no strong target. The children of Israel had defeated stronger enemies in the past. In fact, the men sent to spy out Ai had reported that this would be an easy victory. There was no need to waste the entire army on this enemy. Just send 2000 or 3000 men to fight Ai, they had advised Joshua.

The mini-army was put to flight by a weak enemy. Sinful actions can cause a reversal in the outcome of something that looks like a sure thing. Here was Joshua with dead soldiers and a retreating army. He knew that this news would spread to other enemies they intended to fight. Even with no means of rapid communication in those days, everybody got the news. Nations had heard of the parting of the Red Sea and the Jordan and the defeat of the two kings of the Amorites (Joshua 2:10; 5:1). These were not secrets. Now they would hear that this army was falling to pieces. The weak Ai army had them on the run. Joshua was upset; he was concerned about the future of Israel. He was worried about the reputation of the Lord Himself.

Joshua knew where to go to get answers concerning the surprise, humiliating defeat. He fell on his face before the ark. When things are not going as well as expected, in fact, when they go horribly wrong, it is not a time to visit the psychic or clairvoyant (1 Samuel 28:5-7). It is time to seek the Lord. Where you go when you're in trouble determines if the matter is sorted out or if more trouble comes your way.

Achan had done a clever job concealing the Jericho loot consisting of an attractive garment, silver, and gold. He had buried in his tent something that should have been destroyed, and he also had in his possession things that belonged to the Lord. If you make a habit of holding things that belong to God, you will lose them and much more. He had kept the secret from his fellow soldiers, his leaders, his wife, his children, and his neighbours. But God knew. He had buried the gold, silver, and the garment, but God still saw them. They were covered but still influenced the outcome of the battle. A carefully concealed matter can cause a public disgrace.

Achan acted alone, but his actions affected everyone. Men lost their lives, the army was discouraged, and their leader perplexed. The nation was stunned. The battle after Jericho was Ai. Everything from Jericho was to be left alone. The gold, silver, and brass were consecrated to the Lord before the walls of Jericho fell. Everything else was to be destroyed. This was God claiming first-fruits from the first battle after crossing the Jordan (Joshua 3:16). The actions of Achan caused pain, misery, suffering, and death to himself and his family. He was the man who would not wait, for in the return battle of Ai, God permitted them to take the spoil for themselves. Achan would have had his chance to get gold, silver, and whatever else his heart desired. But he would not wait. He and his family died painful, humiliating, and untimely deaths.

In today's world, men and women who will not wait can suffer the same fate. God says to wait until marriage (1 Thessalonians 4:3). Yet, some will not. They want to enjoy the God-given benefits of marriage without making a commitment. But someone always gets hurt. He says work hard and earn your living (Proverbs 13:11). Yet, some will not. They find it easier to swindle, gamble, rob, and kill to get possessions in a short time. They do not seem to care that these things sometimes represent the hard work of several individuals or of more than one generation.

Our impatience, disobedience, and unwillingness to follow the rule of God can lead to pain, embarrassment, suffering, and untimely deaths, including our own and those around us. This can come through emotional turmoil, incarceration, sexually transmitted diseases, unwanted pregnancies, gun violence, or the judgment of the Lord Himself.

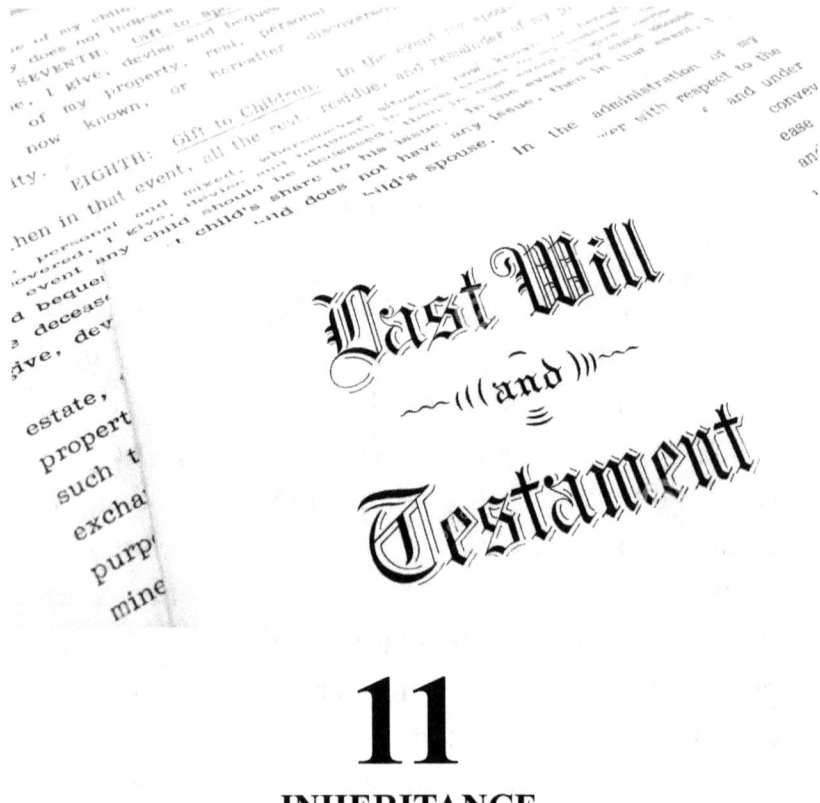

11
INHERITANCE

(Deuteronomy 18)

"... The Lord is their inheritance..."

In our world, acquaintances and family members may promise to leave an inheritance for you, but only under certain conditions, and they are liable to change their minds at any point during their lifetime. Inheritances are received after the person has died. In some cases, this may even be a motive to wish for or actually hasten the person's death. However, there may be some snags to getting an inheritance.

An inheritance can be lost. After someone has passed on, the person in charge of distributing the estate may be dishonest, incompetent, or ill-equipped to do a proper job. Your inheritance can vanish because of poor investments, unfortunate circumstances, or criminal acts. The person who left the inheritance is dead and can do nothing about it.

There may be dissatisfaction. Some persons receive an inheritance with which they are unhappy. Their memory of their loved one is tainted with disappointment. Fighting is a possibility. Some persons fight through the legal system while others, literally, *fight*. Some even enlist the assistance of spiritualists. In any event, it is a process. It takes time to claim and receive an inheritance. It may be paperwork, negotiation, or some type of fighting.

If you trace back to their allotted boundaries (Joshua chapters 12-21), you will see that some of the tribes of Israel lost their inheritance. This resulted from disobedience, open rebellion, and idolatry. Sometimes they were chased away or carried away from their inheritance.

Some tribes of Israel were dissatisfied with the portion of land allotted to them (Joshua 17:16-18; 19:47). Some had a large population or had many cattle; either way, they desired more land. Tribes of

Israel had to fight for their inheritance. It was not handed over on a silver platter. There were many battles. At times, they had to retreat, complaining of a strong, well-armed enemy. It was their inheritance, but from the start, they learned that it would not be easy (Numbers 13:28).

It took a long time for all the children of Israel to get their inheritance (Joshua 18:2-3). Years went by, and the process was incomplete. Some tribes got their inheritance early but left their wives and children behind and went out with the other tribes to help in the battle (Joshua 1:14).

The tribe of Levi received no inheritance among the other tribes, for the Lord was their inheritance. They may have appeared to be disadvantaged, but God made adequate provision for them. They were not destined to become squatters or beggars among the other tribes. They were given cities and fields in every tribe. The tribe of Levi was set apart by God to be ministers and priests. They had been chosen by God to replace the firstborn of Israel (Numbers 3:41). The sons of Aaron were priests (Exodus 40:13-15). The distribution of the Levites throughout the land of Israel was no accident. In this way, the influence of the ministers and priests of the Lord was spread throughout the land.

Similarly, we are priests (1 Peter 2:9), chosen to minister before the Lord. We offer ourselves to the Lord at His altar. Our influence should be seen and felt wherever the Lord has positioned us. We should not seek to form enclaves, to the exclusion of others, for we have been sent into the world and should seek to spread His influence wherever we are.

The inheritance of the Levites was sure. It could not be altered, lost, or stolen in the way that some earthly inheritances could be. The One who gave the inheritance is alive and is well able, watching over His Word to perform it (Jeremiah 1:12). The Lord is always there. No one can remove us from His presence without our approval. No one can take away our inheritance.

In the wilderness, the Levites were responsible for dismantling, transporting, and reassembling the tabernacle. Within the tribe, different families had different assignments (Numbers 3, 4). God is not the author of confusion (1 Corinthians 14:33). There was to be no chaos when the tabernacle was being dismantled, transported, or reassembled. Today, we are still carrying His presence, for we are His temple (1 Corinthians 3:16).

When the temple was built, the Levites had their assigned roles. They kept the gates, sang, played musical instruments, and led worship, and the priests officiated at the altars. Similarly, we have our roles to play in His presence. We cannot neglect our duties.

Included in the inheritance of the Levites was the right and the privilege to minister before the Lord. If a Levite whose family did not live near the temple, or had not served or ministered there, came with a desire to minister, it was his right to do so. There was to be no discrimination against those Levites who had not served before. Once he had the desire and came to the temple, he received all the rights and privileges due to him (Deuteronomy 18:6-8). He was entitled because he had been born into the tribe of Levi.

We have been born into the kingdom of God, and we belong to a special group. It does not matter if your family has a long tradition in the kingdom and you have come from a long line of ministers, or if you are the first one in your family to serve the Lord. The playing field is level. All the rights and privileges accorded to the family of God now extend to you without prejudice.

The Lord is like a cave full of treasure. If you stand just outside the cave and peek in, you will see some stuff, and you may feel satisfied or impressed. If you step in, a lot more is revealed, and as you explore the depth and riches found in Him, you never cease to be amazed at the wealth of the treasure that awaits you. As you go further in, deeper in Him, more and more is revealed to you. You become more and more like Him, finally realizing that He is infinite and that you can never exhaust His provision or fully explore His riches.

Let us claim and possess what belongs to us: His love, mercy, kindness, goodness, and healing. It will take time and effort for us to begin to realise the vastness of His promises. As we explore the riches of His grace and the glory of His presence, let us rejoice, for He is our inheritance.

12

FOLLOW CLOSELY

(Numbers chapters 9-13)

The children of Israel were being led through the wilderness. This was not an aimless journey. Their destination lay somewhere ahead. The place they were going was far better than the place from which they had come. It would be their own, but Egypt had been a slave camp. That place was also far better than where they were now. This was a wilderness, a barren place, and they were going to a land flowing with milk and honey. They were in transition, and that is always a difficult place.

They were travelling at the will of God. He spoke to them by the movement of the cloud of the Lord. When He said to journey, they journeyed, and when He said to rest, they rested. They moved strictly at the counsel of the Lord. Not even Moses knew the itinerary. The Lord and Moses had a special relationship. He spoke directly to him (Exodus 33:11), not in dreams and visions. There was no danger of the message being misunderstood, incorrectly interpreted, twisted around, or altered for personal gain or pride. Moses got the message directly. Yet God chose to keep Moses *in the dark* about travel plans.

God could have told Moses, "You are going to spend two months at this next stop, then we will travel two days and after that, rest for six months." No, God kept His plans to Himself. There were no sneak peeks, no previews. God knew the journey, knew the destination, and also knew His people. He knew their thoughts the same way He knows ours. He knew when they needed to rest. The wilderness was a harsh environment. He knew they had to be taught obedience and submission, for they were naturally rebellious, the way we are sometimes.

Well, this *"travel when I say so"* and this *"rest when I say so"* did not sit well with the people. Human beings like to feel that they are in control, even if they are not. We want to know what's next and when it will happen. The children of Israel had a lot to learn. They were learning to trust God completely. Maybe they wanted to make the decisions, but God was making them for them. Who does He think He is?

We are perfectly capable of guiding ourselves through this wilderness. Why do we have to obey Him – move now, rest now, move again? they thought. They never knew how long the current journey would be. We do not like uncertainty. Yet Abraham, the father of us all, started off on a journey at the command of God. He was unaware of the destination, but he was willing to obey God completely (Genesis 12:1). But the children of Israel complained.

Who does God think He is to have us journey or rest at His instruction? He really expects us to obey Him? He really expects full surrender? Are we just to follow Him like sheep?

Yes!!!

Why?

He is God; He has made us. We did not make ourselves (Psalm 100:3).

So, the people complained, and He heard. That displeased Him. The anger of the Lord was kindled. Here was God leading His people after delivering them, taking care of them, meeting their every need, and what was their response? *To complain.*

The children of Israel would have never survived a wilderness trip on their own, even a short trip, for they lacked discipline. In a harsh, unforgiving environment, discipline is essential. Sometimes, God has to keep a tight rein on us for our own good. They did not appreciate the move of God, the direction of God, the guidance of God, the protection of God, the love of God, the provision of God, or the presence of God. In fact, they seemed to despise it. Hence, complaints arose.

The fire of God burned among them. Those in the uttermost parts of the camp were consumed. The people cried unto Moses, and he prayed for them. The fire was quenched. Some of our troubles come from our own murmurings, complaints, and disobedience. When we get into trouble, we call the same leader to whom the complaints were directed.

Complaining takes time, energy, and effort. When you focus on complaining, it means that you are not following as closely as you should. You fall farther and farther behind. Eventually, you lag so far behind that you have stopped following, and you are not even aware. You become an easy target for the enemy (Deuteronomy 25:17-18). You open yourself to spirits of doubt, unbelief, fear, and rebellion. You can incite others to rebel and even anger the Lord Himself; that carries its own punishment.

Of the twelve spies sent to search out the land, ten of them chose to rebel against the Word of the Lord and encouraged the rest of the congregation to do the same. They never got to live in the promised land. They never got to tell their kids and grandkids stories of how they were the ones sent by Moses to spy out the land. Instead, they all died prematurely in the wilderness, by the hand of the Lord (Numbers 14:37).

The pathway chosen by the rebellious spies differed greatly from that of Joshua and Caleb, who chose to believe the Word of the Lord. Their faith was strong, and they inherited what God had set aside for them (Deuteronomy 1:35-38; Joshua 15:13-14). Joshua and Caleb stood out from the others (Numbers 13:30). They were not popular when they returned from their mission. The people wanted to stone them (Numbers 14:10) because their report differed from those of the other spies. They had seen the same land and were aware of the same Word of the Lord, yet they chose a different path. They enjoyed promotion and length and strength of days and had the distinction of being the only ones remaining of the original congregation to enter the promised land.

It pays not just to follow the Lord but to follow Him closely. Those rewards apply both to this life and to the one to come. For in this life, you will be blessed, healed, and delivered. In eternity, you will be sure of a heavenly home and not run the risk of missing out and being condemned to an eternity without the Lord.

13

THE CHOSEN

(Numbers 17)

A challenge had been made. How could anyone be sure that Aaron and his sons were chosen by God to be priests? The challengers did not think Aaron had a special claim to the priesthood. They believed they could do a better job. It was all going to be put to the test. God Himself would give an answer overnight. Dry sticks were laid out, one for each tribe. Aaron's name was written on the rod of Levi. The test was whose ever rod blossomed overnight would show the chosen one. The contenders were quite confident. In the morning, the truth would be revealed.

Overnight, a dry stick was transformed into a green plant complete with buds, flowers, and fruit. Trees have a rhythm. They have a time when they flower and bear fruit. In some climates, all the trees follow the pattern together. They all flower and fruit at the same time. In tropical climates, different types of trees tend to have their own patterns or rhythm, so if it is mango season, mango trees are bearing fruit.

God is the one who set up the pattern or the rhythm for the trees to follow. But no tree was involved here, only dry rods. They had no root, no support system linked to the ground, and needed no nutrients or water, but Aaron's rod prospered on its own. It is amazing how a life given to the Lord can bloom and prosper even if it seems to lack those things usually considered essential for success in this world. The dry stick or rod did not follow any pattern or rhythm. There was no time. Everything happened overnight. Aaron's rod budded, brought forth leaves, flowers, and fruit in one night. All the natural laws were broken by the One who made them. It showed who was the chosen priest. It was to fulfill purpose. It was not about Aaron or his sons. It was about God. He wanted to show His power. He does not break the laws of nature for fun, to show off, or to make His servant look good. It is all about Him and His will.

Rebels—that is what the challengers were called. He wanted to show the rebels who was in charge. He wanted to show the rebels who He favoured to do His work. It was clearly not them, not with the attitude they possessed. Fruit was produced overnight. A dry rod became fruitful suddenly.

Prosperity can occur suddenly. I do not mean that you will find a bag of money at your bedside or that you will win the lottery. Prosperity is more than money. It can refer to health, well-being, a state of mind, relationships, spiritual matters, or you can come up with an investment idea, a new product, a new recipe, or something new in whatever your field happens to be. Overnight, things can change. New ideas can blossom, and relationships can improve.

A dry stick is now a fruitful branch. No one watered the rod, planted it, or grafted it, but it matured, grew, and prospered. In the morning, nothing was the same with Aaron's rod. Morning is coming. Change is on the way. The night can only last for so long; it must come to an end. It does not matter whether it is a dry bone (Ezekiel 37) or a dry stick; the transforming power of God can bring about change so suddenly and so astoundingly that all will recognise His power. God leaves no doubt in our minds as to who He has chosen to do certain things in His kingdom.

God shows who are the chosen. There is no need to rebel, envy, or murmur against the chosen. The brothers of Joseph envied him so much that they sold him into slavery (Genesis 37). They had no way of knowing that he had been chosen to rescue nations, including theirs. You also have a chosen field. You should ask God to show you what it is.

Aaron and his sons were chosen to be the first priests. God is sovereign. No one should argue about His choices. It is not about us, our looks, our qualifications, our social connections, our money, or lack of it; it is about ***HIM AND HIS KINGDOM***.

14

ASAHEL

(2 Samuel 2)

In the battle just concluded, Abner of King Saul's army had been defeated by David's men and was on the run. The warrior, Asahel, was pursuing a defeated enemy, as are we. Be warned that an enemy, though defeated, can still be powerful and capable of inflicting great damage.

Asahel was young and gifted. He was very

swift on his feet. He was determined and passionate. There was no half-heartedness about him. He was fighting on the right side; that is, he was on the side of the man whom God had anointed to be king of Israel. Asahel was confident. He came from a family of warriors, and he was one of the top thirty warriors in the army (2 Samuel 23:24). His two older brothers were also fighting, and while the eldest was in charge of David's army, the other was chief among three mighty men (2 Samuel 23:18). Asahel had a reputation. He was also the nephew of David.

In his pursuit, Asahel got within speaking distance of the enemy. The others were way behind. Asahel was fast. He was using his gift as he went after the enemy, but your gift can only take you so far.

Abner, the enemy, recognised Asahel. He knew his name and knew his family. The enemy knows us. We usually think that only the Lord knows us and our names. However, so does the enemy. He knew Job, his family, and his business and was determined to bring him down. However, he needed permission from the Lord (Job 1:12).

Asahel seemed to have everything going for him. However, he was going after an enemy who was far more experienced than he was. He was going after a powerful enemy in his own physical strength and giftings. He had no armour, no protection. Even when he was advised by the enemy to get armour, he refused, for he did not think that he would need it. Abner was not really interested in killing this young warrior, with whose family he was well acquainted.

By contrast, our spiritual enemy, the devil, wants to get rid of us, to take us out of the battle for good. He strives to do this by having us switch allegiances or loyalties. He wants us to be on his side so that we are no longer opposing him. In the battle we face today, there are only two sides; so, to reject one side is to automatically support the other.

We are urged by the apostle Paul to put on the whole armour of God (Ephesians 6:11). We need armour as we come up against the enemy. Being partially clad in armour is not sufficient. We need complete protection. Areas left exposed will be seen and targeted by the enemy.

David went up against Goliath and beat him although he had no armour. The giant was clad in armour while David had none, not by choice, for he had never used armour before, and the enemy was waiting (1 Samuel 17). We no longer have that problem. There is spiritual armour for everyone now.

In the fight against Goliath, David had no armour, but he had something else that Asahel lacked. He had the anointing. After the prophet Samuel had anointed David, the spirit of the Lord came upon him from that time (1 Samuel 16:13). When David ran out to meet Goliath, he was not alone; the Spirit of God was with him. Goliath only saw David, who seemed to be an easy target. The giant even felt insulted that the army of Israel had sent this unimpressive, poorly armed youth to fight him (1 Samuel 17:42).

We sometimes underestimate the enemy. Do not believe that you can go up against him on your own. The anointing is necessary. The story of Samson tells us that he was defeated after the anointing left him, unknown to him (Judges 16:20). The anointing is not a permanent fixture for us. We can lose it by our own foolish, ungodly acts. Then our main line of defense is gone.

Asahel was an easy target. He had no armour, and he had no anointing. He was killed with the blunt or dull end of the spear. The enemy hit him hard. The spear went right through him. He died right there, out in the open where all could see. Everyone was shocked. They all knew of his gifting, his passion, and his family connections. No one expected him to be killed like that. They stood still when they came upon his body. His demise was so unexpected that he was not even included in the overall casualty count for the battle, for it was recorded as 19, plus Asahel.

We, too, are shocked when front-line warriors are taken down. It is never done secretly. It is always out in public for maximum effect. The enemy hits them hard, like Asahel. It is not expected. But have they been fighting in their own strength? Have they set aside the armour? If you have to put armour on, then you can also put it aside. Is the anointing of God still on their lives? Was it ever there? In this battle that we are fighting, age is unimportant. Asahel was young, energetic, and vibrant, but none of that was useful when he confronted the enemy.

Your giftings can take you so far and no farther. They are not enough. Passion and determination are not enough, the correct background is not enough, support from family or from a group is not enough, and confidence is not enough. Recognising the enemy is not enough. We need the whole armour of God, and we need the anointing if we are to emerge victoriously.

15

CORRECT OFFICE

(Judges chapters 17-18)

In Judges chapter 17, there is a mother-son squabble about a missing sum of money. It is a large sum, and the matter is settled when the son, Micah of Ephraim, returns it. She is relieved because this sum, she declares, is dedicated to the Lord to make a graven image. God's people have strayed so far away from Him that this is considered perfectly normal.

When you start mixing the practices of the unbelievers with your faith, you get chaos. Actually, you can get strange occurrences all happening in the name of the Lord, like Jephthah sacrificing his own daughter (Judges 11:31-40). Human sacrifice is always an indication of demonic worship since this was never sanctioned by God. As a test, God had asked Abraham to sacrifice his son but was not allowed to go through with it (Genesis 22).

The silversmith did his work, and Micah became the proud owner of a house of gods. He seemed to have gained prominence in the community because of this. He makes one of his sons a priest, and he functions in the role until a Levite happens by and is offered the position.

This Levite, probably not a descendant of Aaron, becomes a priest in a house of idols. Somehow, the newly appointed priest, being a Levite, legitimises the idol worship. The blessings of God are expected to follow. In our world today, we seek to legitimise wrongdoing by having the rich and famous endorse it, practise it themselves, or openly admire and praise those who do. However, the law of God has already been laid down, and He is not going to make exceptions because it has become the cultural norm or the view of the majority of the population. Having a hint, a suggestion, or a slight appearance of normalcy does not make it correct. It remains the same now, as it was back then.

The Levite is being consecrated by an idol worshipper to serve in a house of idols. Micah has no spiritual authority to consecrate anyone. He placed himself in that position because his mother owned a large amount of money that was used to set up a house of gods. Similarly, today, persons with no spiritual authority are doing all kinds of things because they happen to find themselves in a particular position. Aaron and his sons were consecrated by God to be priests (Leviticus 8). Levites were to minister to priests (Numbers 3:6-9).

We need to know the purpose of God for our lives. The Levite actually believed, or at least behaved, as though he was a priest of the Lord, for he gave counsel in His Name. Deception can be contagious. Once it starts to spread, it is difficult to control. The Levite was given a good package, and he was happy until a better offer came along. A passing band of invaders from another tribe came upon the house of gods and the priest, and they could not believe their good fortune. This was too good to leave behind. Here was a house of gods, ripe for the taking, and take it they did. They were impressed with the house of idols while they neglected the true God who was all around them, who had brought their forefathers out of Egypt and had blessed them abundantly.

As they removed the idols and all the trappings, they were challenged by the priest. The offer they made him was so attractive that he gladly went with them. He was being promoted from being a priest to a family and community to being a priest to an entire tribe. He and the gods were relocated to a position of greater influence. Under threat of violence, Micah and his supporters had to give way after pursuing the "*godly thieves.*" God cannot be stolen or forcibly removed from one place to another. For He is all-powerful and present everywhere. Neither can His influence be restricted by geography. Unknown to them, both the invaders and the owners of the house of gods were missing out on quite a lot. For the true God is far more impressive than the workmanship of any craftsman or worker of metals.

The influence of the Levite was growing. There were more people to deceive. Growth and increasing spread of influence are not necessarily signs of the approval of the Lord. The Levites belonged to God (Numbers 3:12,45). They were different from the other tribes. This pretend priest had strayed far away from the purpose of God for his life. Maybe God has singled you out for a particular purpose. You are not free to go off and do whatever you wish.

Do not simply immerse yourself in activities that have a religious appearance. Stay in His will for your life and fulfill your purpose. There can be no greater achievement.

16

SAMSON, THE LOSER

(Judges chapters 13-16)

Samson did not start off as a loser; no one does. He was anointed from the womb, so he actually started off as a winner. He was most likely an only child, but we know that he was the firstborn. His mother, like some others in the Bible, was initially barren until God worked a miracle. Children born under these circumstances were no ordinary children. They turned out to be great, making a huge impact and leaving lasting legacies. They include Isaac (Genesis 17:21), who inherited the blessings of his father Abraham, and Jacob and Esau (Genesis 25:21), who went on to produce great nations. Also included are Joseph and Benjamin (Genesis 30:22), the former rising to become the Prince of Egypt, while the latter produced the first king of Israel. Samuel the prophet was borne by a woman previously barren (1 Samuel 1:11), as was John the Baptist, the forerunner of Christ (Luke 1:7).

Samson was greatly loved by his parents, who had a strong marriage, and both feared the Lord. While Samson was growing up, the environment was not ideal, as the nation was the target of the Philistines, who oppressed them as a result of their disobedience to God. However, his home was spiritually strong, as his parents were anxious to please and obey God. Samson had a spiritual head start. He was specially chosen and anointed by God from the womb. There are not many others like him in the Bible. Other persons were chosen and anointed as adults, for example, the disciples, the apostle Paul, and the Old Testament prophets. A few, like Jeremiah (Jeremiah 1:5) and John the Baptist, were born anointed (Luke 1:15).

The downfall of Samson was that he loved the company of the enemy. He was never interested in the women of Israel. He frequented the land of the Philistines, who were their rulers. If you keep frequenting the club, the bars, the place where strange gods are worshipped, or that website, after a while, it will get to you and get inside you.

Samson made no attempt to wage war against the enemy but only wanted personal revenge as the need arose. He never truly fulfilled the purpose of God for his life, which was to deliver Israel. He used a piecemeal approach as he saw fit that was convenient and personally profitable. He was anointed for a purpose. It was not for personal gain; it never is. God does not anoint a baby or a fetus for no specific reason. It is always for a specific task.

Samson's parents were upset and disappointed when he told them of his first love, a woman of the Philistines. They could not understand why he had not chosen a local girl from his own people. I suppose it can be argued that Samson was being used by God in this matter, for it was He who allowed the attraction. Maybe, this was to serve as an introduction for Samson. When things did not work out as Samson had hoped, the clash of cultures proving too much, Samson could have let the matter end there, but he refused. He pursued it. On and on it went, the need for personal revenge. He never rose above the realm of his personal self-interest. That was what mattered the most to him.

What Samson Lost

1. The first thing Samson lost was his purpose. It was never the intention of God that Samson spend his days venturing into the land of the Philistines

seeking pleasure and adventure. He never acted on what he was supposed to do.

2. Samson lost his desire for the things of God. He was a judge in Israel but set a poor example. People were looking up to him. His interests lay solely in pleasure. A life lived in pursuit of pleasure is one that is full of selfishness. You expect much more from a leader, especially in times of trouble, as was the case in the days of Samson when his people were being oppressed.

3. Samson lost his sense of direction. He went the wrong way. He became caught up in performing and showing what he could do. He boasted, though not verbally, in his great strength. He enjoyed playing games with the enemy, believing he would always come out on top.

4. He lost his hair, but far more importantly, he lost the anointing. He did not even know when it left him. The Spirit of God was so familiar to him that he treated Him with scant courtesy. Samson was all on his own. This was a new experience for him. Now, without the anointing, he was just like any other man. He was not a giant, as were found in other lands. He was just like everybody else. Well, worse actually; because of his former deeds, he was now a special target for the enemy. The enemy could have killed him as soon as he was captured, but that would have been too easy on him. They wanted him to suffer shame and humiliation. They wanted to put him on display as a trophy. The enemy also wants

to do that to us.

5. Samson lost his vision. That was the first thing the enemy took away. When you lose your vision, you can go the wrong way and not know it; you can be easily led, become submissive to the enemy, and do the wrong thing. You cannot see what is important. Things pass you by or slip through your fingers because you have lost your vision.

6. Samson lost his freedom. He was used to roaming around; now, he was confined. The liberty given to us by Christ is precious. Do not allow the enemy to take it away. Samson was bound and became a prisoner. He had to follow the rules of his captors. Had he followed the rules of God, he would have never found himself in that position. He was now working for the enemy against his will when he should have been joyfully working for the Lord and in His will.

7. Samson lost his spiritual identity. His parents knew that he was a gift from God. Now, in captivity, the enemy was seeing him as a gift from their god, thinking that it was his work, but it was Samson's own foolishness that delivered him into their hands. When people saw Samson, they should have been praising God, but now when they saw him, they praised a false god.

8. Samson lost his dignity. He was an object of sport, providing entertainment, performing for the enemy. They were having a good time at his expense.

9. Samson lost his position in society. He had been a judge, in a great position of leadership. Now, he was just a blind captive in the camp of the enemy, being led by a little boy.

10. Samson lost his desire for living and his life. Life became meaningless. He existed without vision that could not be restored. His life could never be the same. He chose death with the enemy when, had things gone differently, he could have lived with the people of God. What a bitter-sweet victory. He snatched some victory from defeat, and this was his final act as he literally brought the house down, killing more Philistines in his death than he did in his life. The greatest memory remaining is that he was a strong man. In reality, he should have had a long, fruitful life, delivered Israel, and become a role model for every little boy in his nation. He died, but the Philistines remained an enemy to the people of God for generations to come.

The failure of Samson to fulfill his purpose affected the entire nation. Let us fulfill the purpose of God in our lives because many others are affected for a long time by our failure to do so.

17

PURITY

(Leviticus 24:1-7)

Usually, when we speak of purity, everyone's thoughts turn to sexual behaviour. However, purity can also be considered in the spiritual sense. That is the type of purity on which we are now concentrating. In the tabernacle, a light was to be left burning all night, and pure olive oil was needed for the light. Olive oil is well-known to us. It is used in our kitchens, on our dining tables, as a cosmetic, and in our churches. It is quite versatile.

Olive oil pressed from the olive fruit was to be pure. No mixtures were to be tolerated. No watering down of the oil was allowed. Some of the juices and other products on the market today have been so mixed to maximise profits for the manufacturers that they are now a far cry from the original. Everything is artificial about them, the taste, and the colour.

Oil is a type of the Holy Spirit. Just as life would have been difficult without the availability of olive oil, our lives would be difficult without the benefit of the guidance of the Holy Spirit. In the tabernacle and later in the temple, oil was needed for the lamps. In our churches today, we need the Holy Spirit to give light, to show us the correct way, to remove the darkness of human-based programs and human wisdom.

There can be no substitute for the Holy Spirit. He alone can do the job. He has no competition. He alone is capable, and there can be no mixtures. Purity is required. But what do we find today? We find a new attitude, a new movement, a new experiment to mix, blend and combine the Holy Spirit with a number of things, a number of ideas, a number of ideologies. Some have attempted to mix the Holy Spirit with a bit of yoga, mindfulness, meditation, and other Eastern philosophies. Also, mixtures with the New Age movement, with personal agendas, and even with other gods have been tried.

When professing Christians, claiming to be full of the Holy Spirit, willingly participate in festivals where other gods are worshipped and have no problem, we know that something is wrong. When Israel strayed from the Lord, they kept just a little of Him and mixed or attempted to mix Him and His worship with that of other gods. But God is a stand-alone God. Strange practices result when we try to mix Him. People commit sin and claim it to be His will.

When you try to mix the Holy Spirit with another spirit of your choice, the problem is that the Holy Spirit is not a mixer. He operates alone. When a mixture is attempted, He leaves, and you are left with only the proposed mixing agent, which expands to fill all the space. You believe He is still there. But He is gone. Purity is essential. It is either 100% Holy Spirit or 0%. It is the Holy Spirit all the time. He does not do part-time work or seasonal work. The olive oil was to cause the lamp to burn continually. It is either the Holy Spirit all the time or none of the time. He will not be put away in a cupboard until you are ready again. He is not like a Christmas tree.

When He sees our unwillingness to be full-time in our relationship with Him, He leaves. Whatever we find more desirable, more attractive, can occupy the most important part of our lives full-time. In our churches, when it is realised that He is gone, a desperate attempt is made to find an impressive substitute. Some churches have not even realised that He has left. Samson also did not realise the anointing had left him (Judges 16:20).

We try to timetable the Holy Spirit and His work. He had better finish whatever He wants to do in the ten minutes or so we have grudgingly allotted to Him. He ought to know when it is time for Him to leave. He has actually left many churches, though they remain full, welcoming, attractive, and entertaining.

It is not possible to have the Holy Spirit perform like a circus clown; *this is the time to do whatever You do, then go away*. But the Holy Spirit is in charge, in control, sitting at the head of the table. Do we really want Him to be in full control of our lives, our churches, and our programs? No, we want Him to show up when it is convenient for us. When we are in the mood, when we can pencil Him in, He needs to make an appointment and keep it.

Pure oil olive was beaten for the light to cause the lamp to burn continually. The Holy Spirit is not decorative and is not there for entertainment purposes. He is there for a divine purpose. He is not to be mixed, blended, or combined. He cannot be substituted or be put on call and pop up when needed. He is a permanent resident, not a visitor.

May He always be welcome in our homes, our

churches, and our lives. He was sent by our Lord to live with and inside us. Let us not neglect to make Him welcome at all times.

18
THE PROVISION OF GOD

(Numbers 11:4-9)

The children of Israel had recently come out of Egypt. There was a mixt multitude with them. The memories of that land were still fresh in their minds and were operating in a selective fashion. They chose to forget the slavery, the abuse of different kinds, the anguish, the pain, and the murder of their baby boys. Male babies were having a tough time making it out of "delivery rooms" alive (Exodus 1:16). When the enemy attacks a people, he always attacks the males first. Though this is a world striving for gender equality and equal rights, there is still something about the males that the enemy needs to destroy before he gets an entire nation or community.

Here were the children of Israel with their selective memories of life in Egypt. They were supposed to influence the mixt multitude, teach them about God and His ways, but it seemed to be working the other way around. The discontent and open rebellion started with the mixt multitude and quickly spread to the entire camp.

"Who shall give us flesh to eat?" (Numbers 11:4).

This was now the primary concern. There was no thanking God for deliverance and for removing the slave masters who had controlled them and their families. Under slavery, they could not make any decisions for themselves. Their lives were controlled by external forces, and that control was enforced violently. The work was tough, and more work had been added (Exodus 5:9). Nothing could be done about it. Only death seemed to provide an escape. Now they were free. But what occupied their minds? What was their greatest wish? They now had a relationship with their God, whom they were free to worship. They had a leader who was close to God and heard directly from Him. Their main desire, though, was flesh to eat. They occupied themselves with the need to satisfy the physical man while ignoring the tremendous opportunity to develop spiritually.

Manna was being miraculously supplied by God. However, they chose to remember the fish, cucumbers, melons, onions, and garlic of Egypt. If you compare these foods to manna, guess which side is going to win? Variety always seems more attractive. It is human to recall the great food and not the misery. The manna provided by God did not come in different shapes, sizes, or flavours. What was so great about manna anyhow? It did not seem to have much of an appearance. It had to be collected and prepared. Manna appeared mysteriously on the ground at night, just like dew. However, dew can be explained with a bit of science, but how does one explain manna?

When God provides something, it usually defies explanation and meets a need completely. In the case of manna, it was wholesome food, absolutely healthy. It was a complete food, well supplied. It may not have had the look or the taste of Egyptian food, but it was what they needed in the harsh wilderness environment. The great food they now recalled had not seemed so great while they ate it in slavery.

A life left behind may seem attractive in hindsight. We may choose to forget the emptiness, the deep pain and guilt, and the complexity of a life lived in sin. The new Christian life may pale in comparison and seem dull and lacking luster. It is the job of our spiritual enemy to keep our hearts yearning for what we left behind in our spiritual Egypt. It is his job to make us view the Christian life with disdain. For he knows that we are in transition, and when we get to our destination, he will no longer be able to influence us. So, he is pulling out all the stops now. Do not fall for his tricks of selective memory. Look ahead, for we are going somewhere, and though the present circumstances may be less than desirable, we have a God who loves us and provides for us daily.

"Our soul is dried away: there is nothing at all, beside this manna, before our eyes" (Numbers 11:6).

Manna? Is that it? God, I expected much better of You. Surely, You can do much better than this.

Why, we can think of dozens of delicious dishes that God can provide. He is the God who created the universe. Gourmet prepared meals are not outside the realm of His power; nothing is.

But manna? Lord, is that the best You can do? You must be joking. I expected better from You. You expect me to be satisfied with that?

Yes!!

Why?

Because I gave it to you, and I know what is best for you at different times in your life and what will serve you best in the future. With manna, you will never go hungry. You will have no vitamin or mineral deficiency. You will be healthy.

Stacked up against the foods of Egypt or against the foods of your expectation, it may not look like much, but God specializes in doing amazing things with things that do not look like much.

A little meal at the bottom of the barrel did not look like much to the widow. After all, there was a famine, and she had a child to feed (1 Kings 17:14), but she, her son, and the prophet never went hungry. A pot of oil was the only thing left to another widow whose husband had left her in debt. She was about to lose her sons (2 Kings 4:1). God saved her from a life of poverty, kept her boys from slavery, and gave them a comfortable life.

The lunch of a small boy was not impressive (John 6:9). It was not even a man's lunch. When his mother was packing that lunch, she had no idea what she was holding in her hands and how many people would benefit from it after it was blessed by the Master.

A bad man on his way to Damascus to persecute Christians did not seem capable of having a positive influence on the body of Christ (Acts 9:1-6). Yet, the apostle Paul continues to influence with his epistles in the New Testament.

A little brother who was more of a brat than anything else did not seem important in terms of saving a mighty nation from the effects of famine – and not just one nation but surrounding nations as well (Genesis 45:5).

Uneducated fishermen on the shores of Galilee did not seem to amount to much (Matthew 4:18), neither did a crying baby boy in a basket on the River Nile (Exodus 2:3).

Three young men facing a mighty king who had the power to throw them into a furnace did not seem impressive (Daniel 3). If anyone looked and sounded impressive, it was the king.

David, a young shepherd boy sent by his father to carry lunch for his older brothers in the army, did not seem poised to make any contribution to the battle (1 Samuel 17:49). In fact, David was anything but impressive.

A baby in swaddling clothes lying in a manger provided no clue as to His true identity (Luke 2:7).

An innocent man hanging on a cross between two thieves saved the world (Matthew 27:38).

It is not what it looks like now. It is the potential contained within. Manna can keep you for years; it can sustain you, and the supply is guaranteed. It can satisfy. But look at it, lying on the ground, waiting to be collected and prepared. It is provided by the Master. Its potential is untold, just like a seed. Seeds never look impressive and can be easily overlooked. A small and simple seed can become a great tree, providing beauty, shelter for animals, shade, and food. An unborn baby is not strong or particularly lovely to look at. However, that baby, given the opportunity to live, can grow into a loving child, a gifted teenager, a mighty leader, a devoted parent, or an adult who changes the world. Sometimes, what looks impressive now turns out to be disappointing. The giant Goliath looked and sounded pretty impressive on the battlefield compared to David. How God can turn the tables!

Do not despise what God has provided. Do not murmur about it. It may not seem to stand up well to other alternatives, but it is different because God sent it. He supplied it. He understands present and future needs. That is why He sent it. He is our Creator, our Saviour, and knows what is best for us. We need to treasure what He sends us.

19
FEAR

(2 Timothy 1:7)

"For God hath not given us the spirit of fear…"

What is Fear?

Fear is a spirit. It is the opposite of faith. If God did not give it to us, why should we accept it and hold onto it? Fear seldom operates alone but attracts other undesirable spirits. The Bible refers to a type of awe, reverence, and respect that we should feel for the Lord. That is not the type of fear being referred to here. Rather, our subject is the paralysing fear, the absence of faith, and the spirit of fear.

We will now look at some Bible characters and the way fear affected them or how they dealt with it, if it ever influenced them at all.

Job

Job was perfect and upright. God boasted on him (Job 1:8). Can God boast on us? Job was careful to offer sacrifices on behalf of his children. He had no Bible, no church, no pastor, no brothers and sisters in the Lord, for it is believed he lived before these things, yet he feared the Lord. He loved God. Today, we have a lot of support that Job lacked, and we tend to take that support for granted. However, Job had been living with the spirit of fear. He feared failure, loss, sickness, and separation from God (Job 3:25).

Job's troubles did not occur because of his fear; we know he was attacked by the enemy. But Job had been living with fear. The enemy had clearly tried to get to him, his family, and his business but failed because God had a hedge about him (Job 1:10). The enemy walks around as a roaring lion seeking prey (1 Peter 5:8). Maybe, all he could do in the case of Job was to instill fear.

Abraham

In Genesis 12:1-3, God promised Abraham great

blessings. Yet, Abraham was besieged by fear of an earthly king, for he convinced himself that Pharaoh would kill him (Genesis 12:12-13). God had promised to make him a great nation, to make his name great, and to bless the entire earth through him. These were the words of God Himself, so there was no room for error or incorrect interpretation. These promises would have failed if Abraham was killed, and since the promises of God cannot fail, there was no way anyone could kill him. Today, there is none like Abraham, the father of many great nations and religions. However, he lied to get himself out of a situation. His fear caused him to lie, to sin.

Isaac

God had already assured Isaac that the blessings of his father Abraham would continue upon him (Genesis 26:3-7). Yet Isaac was so afraid of the king of the Philistines that he lied about his wife. Is fear passed on to our children? This father and son (Abraham and Isaac) found themselves in similar situations, faced the same fear, and told the same lie.

Both had received promises directly from God. Fear can cause us to deny or doubt the promises God has given us. Fear caused the sins of lying and unbelief on His Word.

The Children of Israel in the Wilderness

They had left Egypt in haste, in victory, and in wealth (Exodus 12:31-36), but when they saw Pharaoh and his armies chasing after them in the wilderness, they were terrified (Exodus 14:10). Their fear found an outlet in murmuring, complaining, and rebelling. Fear caused them to become rebellious. Fear made them forget the miraculous delivering power of God.

Fear can cause us to rebel against the leader whom God has appointed. When they were delivered from Pharaoh and his armies at the Red Sea, the spirit of fear remained and manifested itself again when spies were sent out into the promised land (Numbers 13:27-33). Fear caused them to spend 40 years in the wilderness (Numbers 14). Fear caused a whole generation to die without the promise, and even when they finally inherited the land, fear caused some tribes to settle for less than what God was willing to give them (Joshua 17:16). Fear can cause us to miss out on many blessings, suffer needlessly, die in defeat, turn on our brothers and sisters in the Lord, and rebel against our leader and even God Himself. Fear can cause us to ignore the promise of God and can make what we left behind seem more attractive than the Lord.

The Prophet Elijah

In the book of First Kings chapters 18 and 19 are accounts of the experiences of the prophet Elijah. He had just experienced the real power of God when fire fell from heaven and consumed his sacrifice and the barrels of water poured on it. The nation of Israel had been brought to the point where they confessed that God was the Lord. This came after a long period of idolatry. Elijah had killed hundreds of false prophets and prophesied to King Ahab that rain was on its way. This was after years of drought. The rain fell in torrents. Elijah had even outrun the king's chariot—no mean feat.

However, all these accomplishments went downhill when the king's wife threatened to have him killed. Fear gripped him. He panicked, ran away, and hid in a cave. He slipped into depression, praying for God to end his life. He had no wish to die at the hands of those who sought his life but wanted God to do the job. Self-pity overwhelmed him. He whined about being the only true servant of God left in the land. The revelation from the Lord that there were thousands of others must have shocked him. Fear always makes your reality seem much worse than it is. Even if Elijah were the last true prophet left, why would he want God to end his life? Surely it would make more sense for the Lord to send him out to win others. That should have been the goal, especially since the nation was in a state of repentance. Fear causes irrational thoughts and behaviours.

What are you doing here?

That was the question God had for Elijah. Has fear caused us to be in a place where we should not be? God had important work for him to do. He sent him to anoint two new kings and his own successor. Elijah had been so overcome with fear that he had no idea there was so much waiting to be done. Fear can cause us to abort the purpose of God in our lives.

The Early Christians

The early Christians were afraid of Paul, with fair enough reason. However, it seems that they doubted the converting power of the Holy Spirit. The account of the conversion of Paul is given in the book of Acts chapter nine. Fear convinced Ananias that he had to update God on Saul's activities. He seemed to believe that God was not aware of them. The church at Jerusalem was also afraid of Paul, formerly Saul. Barnabas had to introduce him to the other apostles. At the time, they had no way of knowing that he was joining them. Imagine Paul, writer of a large part of the New Testament, almost rejected because of fear. Paul had been chosen by God to minister to the Gentiles, to kings, and to the children of Israel. Fear can cause us to miss a great blessing and to reject the chosen vessels of the Lord.

The Disciples on the Way to Legion

They thought they were going to die, though Jesus was in the boat with them (Mark 4:36-40). Before boarding the vessel, Jesus had told them that they were going to the other side of the lake. He never said anything about drowning. Jesus had to rebuke the wind, the waves, and his own disciples. They only had fear, no faith. Fear occupies the space that should be given over to faith. Fear ignores the previous works of God (for the disciples had seen many great miracles), and it convinces us that this is going to be the end. On the other side of the lake was a man waiting for deliverance (Mark 5:1-20).

The Disciples in the Boat while Jesus Walked on Water

Jesus walked on the stormy sea that was threatening to sink His disciples' boat (Mark 6:48-51). The sea did not calm down because Jesus was walking on it. There are situations in our lives that may remain the same after prayer, but we are strengthened to be on top of things, though they do not change. Jesus came to His disciples walking on the water, but they were so terrified that they did not recognise Him. Fear can cause us not to recognise the move of God in our lives and in our situations. Jesus would have passed them by. Their deliverance almost went right by them. Fear causes us to focus more on the trouble than on the Lord.

Peter

At the trial of Jesus in the Judgment Hall, Peter denied knowing the Lord because of fear and resorted to using obscenities (Mark 14:66-71). Fear can cause us to follow the Lord at a safe distance. We are afraid to become too close for fear of what others may say. Fear can cause us to resort to our old ways and to deny knowing the Lord by our behaviour and our response to situations.

The Result of Fear in Our Lives
- How many marriages never occurred, and how many children were never born?
- How many businesses were never opened or never expanded?
- How many ministries were never revealed?
- How much anointing was stifled, and how many gifts, talents, and abilities remained unused, unopened, and unexplored and have gone to the grave with their recipients?

The parable of the talents in Matthew 25:14-30 is instructive.

Only eternity will reveal how many souls were lost and how many missionary trips never occurred. And what of the many pastors, evangelists, teachers, missionaries, and singers who never found their calling because of fear and remained quietly sitting in church or functioned in other areas?

How many poor decisions have been based on fear? How many careers never got started because of fear? The spirit of fear did not come from God. That does not mean that we rush out and make rash decisions. It does mean that we prayerfully consider what God wants us to do and do it in His Name.

No Fear

David felt no fear as he raced towards Goliath on the battlefield (1 Samuel 17:45), for he was going in the Name of the Lord.

The three Hebrew boys felt no fear as they explained to the king that they had no intention of worshipping the image he had made, and they were prepared to face the furnace if God did not deliver them (Daniel 3:16).

Rahab did not allow fear to stop her from hiding the spies sent out by the children of Israel to view the land of Jericho (Joshua 2:1). She was risking her life to save it later. She not only saved her own life and that of her family, but she also put herself in the genealogy of King David and of Jesus (Matthew 1:5).

John, the revelator, felt no fear on the isle of Patmos. He could have pitied himself, absorbed in his own trouble, but he was in the spirit on the Lord's day (Revelation 1:10). He put himself in the right frame of mind to receive revelations from the Lord, and we have all benefitted.

Fear will cause you to remain in the boat when you could be out walking on the water with Jesus, having a once-in-a-lifetime experience (Matthew 14:28). Fear can make you live a life of a lower quality than God intended. Fear will make you inherit less than you should. Fear will make you see your enemies, whom you can defeat, as giants while you see yourself as a grasshopper (Numbers 13:33).

Be released from the spirit of fear in the Name of the Lord!!!

20
UNANSWERED PRAYERS?

It has been said that all prayers are answered, either with a yes, no, or wait. But let us explore the zone of prayers that seem to be unanswered by God.

Possible Reasons

1. Selfish Prayers and Prayers Which Answers Will Do More Harm than Good

Selfish or self-centered prayers are seldom answered. Praying for a larger home, bigger pay cheque, or newer vehicle, solely to impress your in-laws, neighbours, or friends, are hardly the types of prayers that attract the attention of God.

I knew someone who used his personal vehicle to transport the elderly to church. This was voluntary and was done with joy. His vehicle was small, and he frequently made more than one trip. One day he remarked that he was praying for a larger vehicle to carry more people. I do not know if he got it, but that is an example of an unselfish prayer. Nehemiah prayed for his homeland and his countrymen who were in distress, though he was in relative comfort at the time (Nehemiah 1:4).

The motive or reason for praying a particular prayer is very important. Is it solely for your pleasure? (James 4:3)

The answers to some prayers can lead us to lose our position in God or backslide. Hezekiah prayed for healing from a sickness that was leading to death (2 Kings 20:1-6). He was taken from the point of death and given an extra 15 years of life. These were 15 healthy years of life, for they were a special gift from God. What would we do if we knew exactly when we were going to die? This amazing answer to prayer did not prove to be an enrichment of the spiritual life of Hezekiah. He lost his way. After his recovery, he received visitors from Babylon, and he was so overcome by the attention that he took the opportunity to show off his accomplishments and his possessions.

He was saying, *"Look! I am just like you. I can join the club."*

He never remembered God. His pride got the better of him. He missed an awesome opportunity to speak of the Lord and His goodness. Maybe this would have been the only chance for these Babylonians to hear a king testify of the goodness of God. To whom much is given, much is required (Luke 12:48).

Judgment was pronounced upon Hezekiah's generation and even on his possessions (Isaiah 39). His response was curious. For he knew how to pray and understood the power of prayer, yet he refused to pray about the judgment. He was content because there would be no trouble in his lifetime, and maybe he understood that he had gone too far and saw no further need of prayer. Ironic, though, that the same Babylonians would invade his country after his death and carry off his offspring as well as his goodly possessions. How a word about the power of God could have changed the course of history!

2. Is What You are Praying About Punishment for Sin?

An unpleasant reality, but an all too common one. In Numbers 20, there is an account of Moses losing his sister, Miriam. Then, he was pushed to the limit by the people he led. They blamed him because they had no fresh fruit and no water. Moses was outraged. God told him to gather the people and speak to the rock in front of them to let them witness the water springing out of the rock. In a fit of rage, Moses gathered the people, called them rebels, took the rod, and struck the rock twice. The water gushed out. Judgment was pronounced immediately. Moses would not be given the privilege of entering the promised land. It was a problem of unbelief. Moses hoped God could be dissuaded by prayer, but the Lord was firm (Numbers 27:12-14; Deuteronomy 3:24-26). He even told Moses that He did not wish to discuss it further. No amount of prayer would change the pronounced judgment.

David's sins of adultery with Bathsheba and the murder of her husband brought the judgment of God upon him, though he repented. The baby born of the union got sick and died, though David prayed and fasted for seven days (2 Samuel 12:13-18). God showed His mercy in loving Solomon, the second son born of the union (2 Samuel 12:24).

3. The Enemy is Holding Up Your Answer.

The prayer of Daniel was heard from the first day, but the enemy delayed the answer for 21 days (Daniel 10:12-13). Many times, the answers to our prayers are delayed by the enemy. During this time, we can become frustrated and impatient. Prayer is serious business. The enemy will not sit back and watch as your prayers are answered. Expect some opposition. He will try every trick available to him to stand in your way and make you give up hope.

4. The Answer is Here, but You Have Not Recognised It.

Jesus walked on the stormy seas and would have passed by His troubled disciples (Mark 6:48). Your answer may come in a way that you were not expecting (Matthew 14:26). The saints of God were in deep prayer for the release of Peter from jail while he stood calling at the gate. He had already been released by an angel and was waiting to be let into the house even as they argued that it could not be him (Acts 12:5-16).

5. Cherishing and Holding on to Sin.

This will cause unanswered prayer (Psalm 66:18). You are not trying to get rid of it; you want to keep it. Maybe it feels good, or you think it is a well-kept secret and there is no need to repent.

6. Rebellious Attitude towards God.

Those who deliberately reject the Lord's teachings and refuse to repent may pray in vain (Proverbs 28:9; Isaiah 1:15).

7. We have to Wait for His Timing.

Zacharias and Elizabeth's prayers for a baby seemed to have been unanswered until he encountered an angel in the temple (Luke 1:13). The baby with which God was blessing them was no ordinary baby boy. He was John the Baptist, the forerunner of Christ (Luke 3:16), and his birth had to be perfectly timed with that of Jesus (Luke 1:41). Also, his parents were old and probably not alive by the time he was executed (Matthew 14:10).

8. A Thorn in the Flesh.

The apostle Paul prayed for deliverance from some issue that plagued him. While we do not know exactly what it was, we do know that it bothered him sufficiently for him to pray about it more than once. God did not answer him by removing the issue but by leaving it there and letting Paul know that He had given him the strength to bear it (2 Corinthians 12:7-9).

9. Ill-treatment of Wives.

This may prove a vexing concern for married men, but the truth is, the way you treat and relate to your wife matters. It is so important, your prayer will remain unanswered if your wife is not shown the love and respect she is due (1 Peter 3:7).

For all of us, though, the way we treat others will play a role in our prayer lives and may determine whether those prayers are answered or not.

10. Speaking Untruths about God.

Human beings are upset when you make false accusations against them; so is the Lord. Remember, we were created in His image and likeness (Genesis 1:26). The Lord was unhappy about what Job's friends had said about Him. He would not hear their prayers but heard Job's because he spoke correctly about Him (Job 42:8).

11. Prayer for Others.

The Lord answered Job and restored him when he prayed for his friends (Job 42:10). Sometimes we are so concerned about ourselves and our problems that we forget to pray for others.

Our Lord instructed us to pray (Luke 18:1). The most infamous and wicked king in the Bible, King Ahab, acknowledged his sins, prayed, and God heard his prayer (1 Kings 21:27). It is not a meaningless ritual nor a church-imposed obligation. He expects us to pray, not just when we are in trouble or have a great need. Prayer enriches our lives, brings us closer to God, builds our faith, and gives us a broader view beyond our present circumstances.

Let us pray.

21
VISION

These can be times of anxiety and uncertainty, but we must keep our vision. In this climate of reduced profits for many businesses, and less income or even no income for some workers (Habakkuk 3:17-18) as well as fearful times for others (Psalms 56:3), let us encourage ourselves in the Lord (1 Samuel 30:6). We must keep our eyes on the Saviour, but this is quite impossible if we lose our vision.

The account in 1st Samuel chapter 11, of the attempt of Nahash the Ammonite to conquer Jabesh-Gilead, teaches us a valuable lesson. The men of Jabesh-Gilead put up no resistance. They simply submitted themselves to Nahash and offered to serve him, presumably out of fear. But that was not good enough for the invader. Yes, he would accept their surrender and service, but only on one condition.

He wanted to put out the right eyes of the people. In other words, he wished them all to have distorted vision. They would lose their ability to fight, resist, or rebel, if they ever wanted to do so. The enemy will never be satisfied with just our fear or our surrender; he wants more.

When Samson, the strong man of the Old Testament, was captured by the enemy, the first thing they took away was his vision (Judges 16:21). He was then bound and made to serve the enemy. The loss of spiritual vision marks the start of a downhill trend. In these times, the enemy seeks to put us in a state of fear, to distort our vision, or take it away altogether. Then, we lose our ability to fight, and he can cause us to serve his purpose, focus on the wrong things, and lose our way. *"Where there is no vision, the people perish"* (Proverbs 29:18).

It is difficult, if not impossible, to fight an enemy that we cannot see or recognise. Ask the Americans who fought in Vietnam. In that war, the North Vietnamese, against whom they were fighting, dug a system of underground tunnels and were able to move around without ever being seen. Even when seen above ground, it was impossible to distinguish the North Vietnamese from the South Vietnamese, who were allies to the Americans.

It is easy to focus on our fears and anxieties, but our God continues to reign (Isaiah 9:7). This is not a time to lose hope, to lose our vision, or to shift our focus. Rather, it is a time to stand strong in the Lord, trust Him completely and see the whole picture.

During the earthly ministry of our Lord, opening blind eyes was a frequent miracle (Matthew 9:27; Mark 10:46; John 9:1). Regardless of what we have or do not have, what we have achieved or have not achieved, let us keep our vision. Let us not give in to the enemy who is still walking about, seeking whom he may devour (1 Peter 5:8).

"Be strong in the Lord, and in the power of His might" (Ephesians 6:10).

Let us not shift our attention to fake news, for we have the good news (1 Corinthians 15:1-4). Let us not focus on distractions (2 Samuel 11:2), for there are many at this time, but let us focus on Him, His calling, and His coming.

The inability or unwillingness to "see" the path you or your organisation should take points to a loss of vision. This means that the individual or organisation loses its way, makes no viable plans, and is easily lost.

The year 2020 brought a series of woes. It is ironic since 2020 denotes, in optometry, perfect vision.

Let us keep our vision, our hopes, and our

dreams alive even in the face of seemingly insurmountable odds. Keep trusting the Lord!

22

OBEDIENCE TO GOD

Why is it important to obey God? It is the first stage in our relationship with the Lord. If we refuse to obey Him, we can proceed no further in Him. It is better to obey God than perform rituals, ceremonies, and other displays that may impress onlookers but mean nothing to Him (1 Samuel 15:22). It is a package. Obeying God goes together with loving Him and serving Him. We cannot claim to love Him and want to serve Him yet refuse to obey Him (John 14:15).

Obedience brings salvation and other blessings (Deuteronomy 11:27; Hebrews 5:9). Disobedience invites His judgment (Deuteronomy 11:28; 1 Samuel 12:15). Once we recognise Him as Lord, it is only natural to obey Him (Luke 6:46).

The destiny of other persons or even future generations may be tied up in our obedience or disobedience. Noah obeyed God (Genesis 6:14) and saved his family. Abraham obeyed God (Genesis 12:1-4), and we have all benefitted. Moses obeyed God (Exodus 3) and led the children of Israel out of Egypt. Jesus obeyed, setting the perfect example (Philippians 2:8; Hebrews 5:8).

The prophet Elijah provides us with valuable lessons in obedience to God (1 Kings 17). After Elijah prophesied to King Ahab about a coming drought, God sent Elijah to the brook Cherith. There, ravens brought the prophet his meals twice a day. These meals, plus water from the brook, sustained Elijah until the brook fell victim to the drought and dried up. *Ravens.* Of all the birds available to the Master, ravens were chosen to bring meals. God made all the birds. Surely, He could have made a more suitable choice. Ravens are not songbirds, pet birds, or even desirable birds. They are not beautifully coloured as some other birds. They feed on dead flesh. But, ravens were quite suitable, if you think about it. They are strong enough to carry a man's food, and they do not attract much attention.

Some of us have lost our blessing, rejected what

God was trying to give us, missed the message, or had the opportunity slip through our fingers because the carrier or the messenger did not meet our approval. God is sovereign. He can choose the unusual, the unwanted, and the less than socially acceptable to bring us the blessing He desires to give us.

Why use birds at all? God is God. He could have caused the meals to miraculously appear at the appropriate times. He could have changed the sand, pebbles, or rocks near Elijah into delicious meals if He so desired. Even the devil knows that there is no challenge there for God (Matthew 4:3). Yet He chose birds. *Why?* This is one of the beautiful features of sovereignty. God can do whatever He wishes. We have to remember this the next time we question, grumble, and murmur about what God is doing in our lives.

The brook Cherith dried up. The prophet Elijah lost his source of water during a drought which was in progress at his command. He had to move on. God had already made the provision before the problem arose. Couldn't God have kept the brook flowing despite the drought? Yes, He could, but Elijah would be used in another place to bring a blessing to a widow who really needed it.

There must have been persons of means living in that area, but God chose a widow. The place where the widow lived was part of the territory belonging to the family of King Ahab's wife. Ahab himself was an evil king who married an even more evil woman who worshipped a prominent false god.

The widow to whom Elijah was sent had only enough food for one meal for herself and her young son. Death was beckoning. In her desperate situation, God spoke to her and commanded her to feed His prophet. Was God seeking to place a financial burden on a widow who was in need herself? She needed someone to give *her* something, but God sent someone who demanded what she needed: food.

Sometimes, God instructs us to give something we need for our own use. We may look around and think that other persons are more capable than we are. Why is God choosing us? We love to question and figure out what God is doing. But His ways are higher than our ways (Isaiah 55:9), and they are past finding out (Romans 11:33).

This widow took up the challenge to obey God and saw a miracle day after day. Her food never ran out. She continued feeding her house guest, and one day, her son became sick and died. The prophet was on the spot to pray for the child. His life returned. One act of obedience ensured blessings of food and new life. One act of obedience can bring a lifetime of multiple blessings. The reverse is also true.

God sent Elijah back to King Ahab to signal the end of the drought (1 Kings 18). This dry spell was to end in the same way it had started—by the word of God's prophet spoken to an evil king. Elijah obeyed God. Perhaps, it would have been understandable for Elijah to refuse to go and speak to Ahab. Who wants to speak to a king who wants you dead?

Ahab had been hunting for Elijah for years, even in foreign nations. All the while, Elijah lived quite comfortably, it seemed, in the land of the family of the king's wife. God knows how to protect His people. He knows the best hiding places, even those that make no sense to us. On the way to the meeting, Elijah encountered Obadiah, the governor of Ahab's house. During the reign of an evil king and queen, here was a high official serving God.

There are persons serving God in the most unlikely places and situations.

Obadiah recognised the power of God and had rescued many of His prophets from death at the hands of the queen. We need more high-ranking public officials who fear God and recognise His power. Obadiah was sent by Elijah to tell the king of his whereabouts. The official resisted at first, knowing that God was able to keep hiding His prophet, then he was finally convinced.

Ahab and Elijah were now face-to-face. Ahab sought to lay blame for the drought and resultant famine at the feet of Elijah when it was the king's own idol worship and evil ways that were the real causes. So, too, in today's world, many seek to blame others for misfortunes when it is their own evil ways that caused the trouble.

Elijah asked Ahab to assemble to Mount Carmel all of Israel and hundreds of false prophets of Baal. There, Elijah successfully offered a burnt offering in spectacular fashion. The prophets of Baal failed miserably and were all killed. All this time, Ahab made no attempt to stop the proceedings. He seemed to have an almost child-like curiosity about God and His power.

When told by Elijah to have a meal, again, Ahab obeyed. After the sighting of a tiny cloud arising from the sea, the message was sent to Ahab that rain was on its way and that he should leave quickly before the rainstorm began. Again, Ahab did what he was told. He did not protest or wield any of his authority as king. Ahab seemed to have a personality that made him easily led. Had his queen been God-fearing, no doubt everything in his life would have been quite different.

Ahab's reaction to the display of God's power was so different from that of his wife. She became more resolute in her efforts to kill the prophet (1 Kings 19:1-2). Mighty acts of God, witnessed by the unbelieving, solicit different responses. Some believe, some wait to see what comes next, while others become more determined in their evil ways.

Elijah should have been riding high on faith. He had proven who was the true God. It was the God of heaven, not Baal. The heart of Israel had been turned back to the true God. The false prophets had been killed. In reality, the queen, worshipper of Baal, should have been hiding from Elijah, but the position was reversed. Here was the mighty prophet hiding in a cave (1 Kings 19).

God saw him running from the queen and heard his request to die. He even sent an angel to feed him. It is a good thing God does not answer all our prayers. God was watching as he found the cave, entered it, and hid. Previously, when God had selected the hiding place, Elijah lived in a loft with his own bed (1 Kings 17:19). Now he was hiding in a cave.

Actually, when God hid the prophet, it was a time to hide. Now Elijah was hiding on his own when it was time to be out in the open doing the work of the Lord. God called him. He answered but felt he needed to update God on the latest; he tried to justify his hiding when questioned by Him. He did this on two occasions until God sent him on a mission to anoint not one but two kings of different nations and anoint his successor. Elijah obeyed.

When God has work for us to do, we should not allow fear to tie us down and make us hide. Step out and do what He has asked.

Elijah went on to outlive both Ahab and his wife and continued in the role of a prophet during the reign of Ahab's son.

When Elijah left this earth, it was in a ride of glory. He did not die at the hand of Ahab's wife, nor did he die alone in defeat and in fear in the wilderness. In fact, he did not die at all. He would have missed out on a ride from earth to heaven in a chariot of fire (the only human being to exit the planet in that fashion) had he disobeyed God.

How many things have we missed out on because of our disobedience? It is better to obey God than men (Acts 5:29). There is no substitute for obedience to God. Obey Him and enjoy His blessings of peace and healing. Nothing beats the satisfaction of knowing that what you are doing is in obedience to Him.

23

DRY BONES

(Ezekiel 37:1-10)

Ezekiel chapter 37 starts off more as the backdrop for a horror movie than anything else. If the Spirit of the Lord had to take us someplace, we would prefer to be taken to a place of gorgeous scenery and delightful foods. The prophet Ezekiel finds himself in a valley of very dry bones.

A dry bone is the final point. This is a situation

where hope has long gone. All dreams of recovery, rejuvenation, and restoration have been eroded. This is the end of the road. When we find ourselves in dry bone situations, despair, depression, and desperation are all that remain; there is a temptation, a tendency to think and to say that not even God can do anything about it.

The famine in Samaria was grim (2 Kings 6:25-33). Normal decent people had resorted to cannibalism and were not ashamed about it. The king's aide assessed the situation using human logic and reasoning and concluded that not even God could fix it. That thought may be excusable given the situation, but it was uttered after the prophet of the Lord had declared otherwise (2 Kings 7:1-2). The Lord's word came to pass as it always does. The unbelieving official met a sorry end.

God has given us all a measure of faith (Romans 12:3), and like all fathers who give gifts to their children, He expects us to use it.

A dry bone situation is very bad. When all those around you are in the same position, there is a prevailing atmosphere of doom and finality. If all your associates are in the same seemingly hopeless situation as you are, some comfort may be derived from the fact that everyone is *just like me*. However, that does not take away from the fact that the entire landscape is filled with hopelessness.

In addition to those bones being very dry, indicating that they had been in that state a long time, they were in a valley. It is not just that the personal circumstances are grievous and those around are in the same position; the entire situation is dismal. Valleys are low places, the opposite of mountains or hilltops. They are not associated with feelings of exhilaration or accomplishment. No one boasts of being in a valley. There is no admiration associated with that environment. Rather, one may be pitied, even ridiculed, for everyone is certain of the finality of the situation.

But God specialises in handling hopeless cases. The Bible carries many examples of His intervention in cases already deemed beyond remedy. Abraham was childless, and he and his wife were advanced in years. But he had a promise of a son from the Lord, and that promise did not expire (Genesis 17:1-6; 21:2). It did not become invalid as the years went by.

Naaman had a brilliant military career but had an incurable disease whose progression would render him unable to perform his duties (2 Kings 5). Then the Lord intervened.

The widow of Nain, having already lost her husband, was faced with the loss of her only son (Luke 7:11-15). The community mourned with her but could not help her recover her loss. Then the Lord intervened.

God breathes life into dry bone situations. He brings order, renews hope, transforms, and empowers. There is a complete reversal that is extreme and difficult to imagine. In the vision of Ezekiel, the dry bones were transformed into a mighty army. Their previous state indicated untapped potential, unused talents and abilities, and unrealised goals. Positioned side by side, one situation is the opposite of the other.

Allow God to take charge of your dry bone situation. He is an expert in that area. He created the heavens and the earth out of nothing (Genesis 1). From the chaos and lack of order on the early earth, He called forth air, light, oceans, and dry land and populated them with plants and creatures. This was done by the power of His Word. In the vision of Ezekiel, it is the Word that brought about the transformation.

What can the Word bring about in your life? His Voice is powerful (Psalm 29). Allow His Voice to speak into your issues, particularly the hopeless ones. Some may believe that dry bones are best kept buried, hidden, but in this vision, these bones lay exposed for all to see. Maybe your dry bone situation is concealed from public view, or maybe it is exposed. Whatever the situation, even though hidden from men, it is exposed to God.

His Word in a dry bone situation brings forth life, for He is the resurrection and the Life (John 11:25).

24

THE JOURNEY OF JONAH

(Jonah chapters 1-4)

Jonah correctly advised King Jeroboam, the son of Joash, about recapturing conquered territory (2 Kings 14:25-29). That went down as one of that king's major accomplishments. The counsel came from the Lord. Jonah was a prophet of God.

God spoke to him about a mission to Nineveh, but it did not meet his approval. Jonah only intended to obey God when he agreed with what God was saying. He tried to flee from the presence of God, but he should have known better. For there is no escaping His presence (Psalm 139:7).

Jonah chose an alternate destination, not the one to which God had sent him. He found a ship going to Tarshish, paid the fare, and boarded the vessel. This *"avoiding God"* was going to be easy, he thought. If God had sent Jonah to Tarshish on some mission that was not Jonah-approved, Jonah no doubt would have selected a vessel heading elsewhere.

Jonah settled down into a deep sleep. Running from God can be exhausting. The prophet needed his rest. A violent storm arose. Jonah slept on. The sailors grew afraid. They resorted to praying to their strange gods while the servant of the true God lay asleep. Jesus slept while a storm terrified His disciples on the Sea of Galilee (Mark 4:37), but that storm had been conjured up by the enemy. When a storm scares those who spend their lives at sea and know the sea well, fear seems justified.

Jonah was awakened by the captain, who could not believe that anyone would be so callous to sleep while lives, including their own, were in danger. The mariners were convinced that this was no ordinary storm. It must have been caused by someone on board. Storms brought on by spiritual forces are no ordinary storms. Whether caused by the enemy or by the Lord Himself, these storms are extreme and command the attention of all, both disciples and those who do not believe in the true God.

Lots were cast onboard the vessel to discover the culprit. Jonah was identified and interrogated. Now the men were really terrified, not just of the storm, but of God from whose presence Jonah fled.

For Jonah, the solution was simple: "*Just throw me overboard,*" he told them.

Though these men did not know the Lord, they had a good idea of right and wrong and valued human life. For God has placed within us a compass that steers us in the right direction, even if we are not in a relationship with Him. Jonah was willing to sacrifice himself to spare the lives of the sailors.

Even then, he expressed no regret about disobeying God and wanting to have his own way. He probably consoled himself that anything was better than going to Nineveh, even untimely death. He was going to have the final say. The sailors made a last-ditch effort to get to land, but the sea fought back. Finally, after praying, asking mercy and forgiveness from a God they did not know, they threw the disobedient prophet overboard. Immediately, the sea calmed. This greatly impacted these men whose lives would never be the same. Jonah's life would also never be the same, for he was in for the ride of his life.

God had sent him to Nineveh, and that was where he was going. Surely, Jonah would have appreciated a more comfortable means of transport. Now he was going *by fish*. Jonah spent three days and three nights in the belly of the large fish and came to his senses, crying out to God for mercy, even waxing poetic. He landed on the shore amidst vomit. An unpleasant and scary journey came to an end. By now, Jonah was more compliant. God picked up exactly where He left off. The instruction had not changed but was issued the second time. There would be no escape. God is sovereign. He could have sent another messenger, for God is never backed into a corner with no alternatives. God decided that Jonah was going to Nineveh, and that is where he went. God should never have to give us the same instruction twice. Initial obedience is best.

Grudgingly, Jonah went to Nineveh, a rather large city. He proclaimed God's Word. The people repented, from the king in the palace to the man in the street. No judgment of God fell upon them. But Jonah, safe from his vantage point outside the city, expressed his dissatisfaction. After his adventurous detour, you would think Jonah's attitude would be different.

God had demonstrated to Jonah His power over nature in the storm, His mercy in delivering him from the storm waves and the large fish and sparing the city of Nineveh, His creative power in preparing a plant to shade him from the sun, and His destructive power as He prepared a worm the next day to devour the plant. The weather grew uncomfortably hot, and Jonah, suffering in the heat, desired death. The Lord actually tried to reason with Jonah about his being so upset concerning the destruction of the short-lived plant to which he had contributed nothing. He compared it to the well-populated city filled with not just adults responsible for their own actions but also with infants and livestock.

We, too, should be concerned with life created by God. His Son died for the most unlikeable, unlovable, and undeserving souls. Who are we to demand God severely judge our enemies while showing us mercy?

Let us not have the attitude of Jonah.

25
RELEVANCE

(Proverbs 3:1-2)

Keeping the Word of God, that is, obeying Him, is not just a spiritual matter. It extends into everyday life. One who observes His sayings can be spared many of the challenges brought on by ignoring what He says. Those who obey God are more likely to live to an old age, which in itself may not be regarded as a blessing, depending on the circumstances.

However, a long productive life with a spirit of contentment is admired by all. Lives can be cut short because of poor lifestyle choices, e.g., substance abuse and sexual promiscuity.

How many young and not-so-young lives have been lost due to drug overdoses, alcoholism, smoking, and vaping? Not only are there direct consequences to those who practise these, but to their families, co-workers, employers, fellow motorists, and other users of the road. Families, companies, and countries spend millions each year on rehabilitation, advertisement campaigns, health care, insurance, legal matters, and therapy. Work hours are lost, and many careers are cut short, while many never see the light of day. Those imprisoned by substances are constantly on the hunt for satisfaction.

Some human beings still believe they can substitute things for the presence of God. Nothing beats His presence. No high induced by any substance can be measured to the one supplied by the Most High. He made us, knows exactly how we are wired and what we are wired for, yet we behave as if He is a doting grandfather out of touch with reality.

Sometimes, it may look as if God had a plan to take all the fun out of life with His laws concerning sex and marriage. They may not be popular now but keeping them would eliminate issues such as teenage pregnancy, extramarital affairs, sexually transmitted diseases, prostitution, sex trafficking, and bestiality.

So many issues we face today are the direct consequences of disobeying the Word of God. Certain cancers and other diseases, some divorces, many instances of domestic abuse, and financial hardships can be traced back to disobedience of the law of God.

Trying to recreate the Garden of Eden in nudist colonies will never work. The initial disobedience that occurred there continues to spread its effects. Discontentment and the search for something better in an environment where everything has been supplied, rebellion against authority, the belief that someone who truly loves you is holding out on you, greed, and the urge to want more though you have it all, are all offshoots from the Garden of Eden.

Submit to God and His Word and become a better person, not a super-human who makes no mistakes, but one who recognises where his strength lies and, consequently, one who surrenders it all to God.

26
FIRST AND ONLY

"In the beginning God created the heaven and the earth" (Genesis 1:1). These are the first words in our Bible. They set the tone for the rest of His Holy Word. He is the beginning. He always was and is and is to be (Revelation 1:8). That sense of permanence or eternity is difficult for our human minds to grasp. He is the only God who can claim to have created the heavens, earth, and everything in them.

Other gods have come on the scene, and their

popularity has waxed and waned over time, from region to region and age to age. The names of some gods are now only to be found in the pages of history. Some will never even be known as their followers are no longer on the scene.

Our God, the only God who loves and cares for His people, remains relevant, powerful, and touched by our issues, and His followers continue to increase. Many campaigns have been launched over the years to obliterate His Name and memory from human history, but today, the leaders of those campaigns have faded, and He and His Word remain as powerful as ever.

For thousands of years, many efforts to destroy His Word, or make His followers doubt it, have been tried. Starting in the Garden of Eden, when the serpent twisted around the Word of God to convince Eve to take the bait (Genesis 3:5), those attempts continue in our modern world. Since God Himself and His Word are indestructible, the next option pursued is to distort or to instill doubt.

One king burned the written Word of God (Jeremiah 36:23), but as he discovered, the pages could be burnt, but the Word could not. Throughout history, copies of the Bible have been banned and burnt, but the Word of God endures forever (Isaiah 40:8). He is the only God whose Word cannot be destroyed and was actually made flesh and lived among us (John 1:14).

Since God the Father is eternal and indestructible, so is His Son. He is the first and only God to send His Son to earth to redeem humankind. His sinless Son was treated as a common criminal and suffered a humiliating death on a cross. For a while, it looked like the enemy had finally won, but the perceived victory was snatched away on Resurrection morning. There had been previous raisings from the dead (2 Kings 4:35; 13:21; Luke 7:15; 8:55; John 11:44), but this was the first time the Resurrected One would never die again (Revelation 1:18).

Jesus was the only One who was qualified to rescue mankind from sin, being made one of us and being sinless Himself. In Him, we have help, hope, peace, joy, prosperity, and abundance. He is preparing a place for us (John 14:3), something no other god is doing. Our God desires us to share eternity with Him. No other god has expressed that desire; in fact, only our God will endure through eternity.

Throughout history, we can find examples of gods who failed miserably and were thrown into the fire (2 Kings 19:18), otherwise destroyed, or condemned to be isolated to the confines of history.

Jesus was the first and only baby ever born to a virgin (Matthew 1:18; Luke 1:34). He was a firstborn son who lived up to His responsibility towards His mother, even in the middle of His suffering (John 19:26-27).

During His earthly ministry, Jesus attracted great crowds, being the first to teach with such authority and perform such miracles (Matthew 7:29;

John 7:46). He was also the first to have great power in His Name (Luke 10:17; Philippians 2:10).

Jesus rode into Jerusalem using a colt on which man had never sat (Luke 19:30). After His death, the tomb in which He was placed was brand new (Luke 23:53). Jesus takes no delight in second place. He is and must always be first.

In Egypt, the death angel slew the firstborn (Exodus 12:29). The firstborn son of each family of Israel belonged to God (Exodus 22:29) and was supposed to be the priest of their family. After the chaos involving the worship of a golden calf, God chose the tribe of Levi instead of all the firstborn (Numbers 3:41), after they were the first to declare allegiance to the only true God (Exodus 32:26).

The feast of firstfruits (Exodus 34:26) reminds us of the importance God places on being first. When we receive our salaries and profits, the Lord's money is to be taken out first (Proverbs 3:9). The feasts of Passover and Unleavened Bread, which foreshadowed the crucifixion of our Lord, the shedding of His blood, and the removal of our sins, were celebrated in the first month (Numbers 9:5).

Our God, who is eternal, has revealed what is to take place in the end times, and His Word is proving to be true, despite attempts to twist, distort, and doubt it.

Our God, First and Only!

www.ingramcontent.com/pod-product-compliance
Lightning Source LLC
Chambersburg PA
CBHW070913080526
44589CB00013B/1276